AFRICAN WORLD HISTORIES

Transatlantic Africa
1440–1888

AFRICAN WORLD HISTORIES

Series Editor:
Trevor R. Getz, San Francisco State University

African World Histories is a series of retellings of some of the most commonly discussed episodes of the African and global past from the perspectives of Africans who lived through them. Accessible yet scholarly, *African World Histories* gives students insights into African experiences and perspectives concerning many of the events and trends that are commonly discussed in the history classroom.

Titles in the Series

Published

Cosmopolitan Africa, 1700–1875
Trevor R. Getz, San Francisco State University

Colonial Africa, 1884–1994
Dennis Laumann, University of Memphis

Transatlantic Africa, 1440–1888
Kwasi Konadu, The City University of New York, and Trevor Getz, San Francisco State University

Africanizing Democracies, 1980–Present
Alicia Decker, Purdue University, and Andrea Arrington, University of Arkansas

Forthcoming

Sovereignty and Struggle, 1945–1994
Jonathan T. Reynolds, Northern Kentucky University

Bantu Africa
Christine Saidi, Kutztown University; Catherine Symone Fourshay, Susquehanna University; Rhonda M. Gonzalez, University of Texas at San Antonio

AFRICAN WORLD HISTORIES

Transatlantic
Africa
1440–1888

Kwasi Konadu

The City University of New York

Epilogue by Trevor R. Getz

New York   Oxford
OXFORD UNIVERSITY PRESS

It furthers the University's objective of excellence in research,
scholarship, and education by publishing worldwide.

Oxford   New York
Auckland   Cape Town   Dar es Salaam   Hong Kong   Karachi
Kuala Lumpur   Madrid   Melbourne   Mexico City   Nairobi
New Delhi   Shanghai   Taipei   Toronto

With offices in
Argentina   Austria   Brazil   Chile   Czech Republic   France   Greece
Guatemala   Hungary   Italy   Japan   Poland   Portugal   Singapore
South Korea   Switzerland   Thailand   Turkey   Ukraine   Vietnam

Copyright © 2015 by Oxford University Press

Published by Oxford University Press
198 Madison Avenue, New York, New York 10016
http://www.oup.com

Oxford is a registered trademark of Oxford University Press

Library of Congress Cataloging-in-Publication Data
Konadu, Kwasi, author.
African world histories : Transatlantic Africa, 1440–1888 / Kwasi Konadu,
The City University of New York ; epilogue by Trevor R. Getz.
pages cm
Includes bibliographical references and index.
ISBN 978-0-19-976487-7
1. Slave trade--Atlantic Ocean Region--History. 2. Slave trade--Africa--History.
3. Slavery--Atlantic Ocean Region--History. 4. Slavery--Africa--History. 5. African
diaspora--History. I. Getz, Trevor R., writer of added commentary. II. Title.
III. Title: Transatlantic Africa, 1440–1888.
HT1322.K66 2014
306.362091821--dc23

2013046090

Printing number: 9 8 7 6 5 4 3 2 1

Printed in the United States of America
on acid-free paper

CONTENTS

Maps and Figures

MAPS

FIGURES

Acknowledgments

Mpaeɛ. Onyankopɔn, Asase Yaa, abosompɛm, nananom nsamanfoɔ, m'abusuafoɔ, meda mo ase pii. Na monim sɛ meresua, momma menhu da biara. To Ronnie (Amma), Abena, Sunkwa, and Afia, *ɔdɔ yɛ dɛ te sɛ ahwedeɛ.* Beyond my family, there are a number of people to whom I owe a debt of gratitude. For their kind response to queries about source materials on the topic of this book, special thanks are due to Edward Alpers, Mariana Candido, Paul Jenkins, Adam Jones, Ole Justesen, Ray Kea, Jon Miller, Dylan C. Penningroth, and John Thornton. For helpful and encouraging conversations over the years, let me register my thanks once more to Kofi Baku, Boubacar Barry, Scot Brown, Clifford Campbell, George Cunningham, Dianne Diakité, Kwame Essien, Fallou Ngom, Dane Peters, Paula Saunders, Mwalimu Shujaa, Andrew Smallwood, James Turner, and Kwesi Yankah. I also am grateful for the insightful critiques of the manuscript provided by Paul Lovejoy, Hilary Jones, and Ibrahim Hamza. Finally, I thank Trevor Getz, the series editor, for the opportunity; Charles Cavaliere and his staff at OUP; and I thank you, the reader, for choosing this book. The usual disclaimers apply.

About the Author

Kwasi Konadu is Associate Professor of History at The City University of New York. He has conducted extensive archival and field research in West Africa, Europe, Brazil, the Caribbean basin, and North America, and much of his writings focus on African and African diasporic history and indigenous sources. He is the author of *Indigenous Medicine and Knowledge in African Society* (2007), *A View from the East: Education and Cultural Nationalism* (2009), *The Akan Diaspora in the Americas* (Oxford University Press, 2010), *The Akan People: A Documentary Reader*, 2 vols. (2013), and (with Clifford Campbell) *The Ghana Reader: History, Culture, Politics* (forthcoming). Dr. Konadu is also the founding director of the nonprofit educational publishing group, Diasporic Africa Press, Inc.

Series Introduction

The volume that you hold in your hands is an interpretation of the history of the Atlantic slaving system from the perspective of Africans themselves. I say this as the editor of the *African World Histories* series, a new approach to teaching and learning for African History and African Studies courses. The main objective of the series is to approach African and global experiences from the perspectives of the Africans who lived through them. By integrating accounts and representations produced or informed by Africans with accessible scholarly interpretation in both local and global frameworks, *African World Histories* gives students insight into Africans' understandings and experiences of such episodes as the Atlantic slave trade, the growth of intercontinental commerce, and the Industrial Revolution, colonialism, and the Cold War. The authors in this series do this by looking at culture, politics, social organization, daily life, and economics in an integrated format using the most recent studies as well as primary source materials. Unlike many textbooks and series, the authors of *African World Histories* actively take positions on major questions like the centrality of violence in the colonial experience, the cosmopolitan nature of precolonial African societies, and the importance of democratization in Africa today. Underlying this approach is the belief that students can succeed when presented with relatively brief, jargon-free interpretations of African societies that integrate Africans' perspectives with critical interpretations and that balance intellectual rigor with broad accessibility.

As the author of this book, Kwasi Konadu has produced a text that focuses not on the mechanics or operation of the Atlantic slaving system, but rather on the beliefs, ideas, and worldviews of the Africans who experienced it. His interpretation brings narratives produced by Africans to readers and interprets them through a process of painstaking research and rich contextualization. My own contribution to this volume is limited to the epilogue, which focuses on questions of memory and heritage.

Many texts have been published that interrogate some aspect of the transatlantic slave system, and many scholars have contributed to our understanding of its operation and impact. Edward Reynolds, Philip Curtin, Basil Davidson, and Joseph Inikori wrote or edited several of the classic texts on the subject. David Northrup and Lisa Lindsay both have succeed in bringing narrative and context to the classroom. David Eltis and David Richardson have led a massive project to quantify the system. Suzanne Miers has brought the field forward to include the twentieth century. Martin Klein, Sandra Greene, Alice Bellagamba, and other scholars have led efforts to bring together research on the voices of the enslaved. In parallel effort, Paul Lovejoy, Chandler Saint, and their colleagues have focused on individual biographies. Ugo Nwokeji, Walter Hawthorne, Gwendolyn Hall, Edmund Abaka, and a host of others have proposed answers to questions of how identity and culture were transformed through the system in Africa, the Americas, and the Atlantic. Ismail Montana and Choiki El Hamel have broadened the conversation to include North Africa in this period. Joseph Miller has been both a contributor to all of these debates and the annalist of the field as a whole.

Kwasi Konadu's unique interpretation of the words left behind by Africans who experienced this system, exemplified in this volume, both draws from these sources and provides a unique perspective to any reader. Konadu's focus is on the perspectives and messages produced by Africans of this period and what they tell us about broad paradigms and worldviews in Africa and the Atlantic during the long period in which the system operated. As such, he pulls together individual autobiographies and other accounts to gain insight into broader systems of thought. Moreover, he does not seek to be uncontroversial but rather to push the boundaries of our academic and societal approaches to understanding this system and its human impact.

Like other textbooks in the *African World Histories* series, this one is designed for use in both the World History and the African History/Studies classrooms. As an African History/Studies teaching tool it combines continent-wide coverage with emphases on specific, localized, and thematic stories that help demonstrate wider trends. As an auxiliary text for the World History classroom, the volumes in this series help to illuminate important episodes in the global past from the perspectives of Africans, adding complexity and depth as well as facilitating intellectual growth for students. Thus it will help world history students understand not only that the human past was "transnational" and shared but also that it was perceived differently by distinct groups and individuals.

African World Histories is the product of a grand collaboration. The authors include scholars from around the world and across Africa. Each volume was reviewed by multiple professionals in African history and related fields. The excellent team of editors at Oxford University Press, led by Charles Cavaliere, put a great deal of effort into commissioning, reviewing, and bringing these volumes to publication. Finally, we all stand on the shoulders of giants in the field like A. Adu Boahen, Joseph C. Miller, Chiekh Anta Diop, Joseph Ki-Zerbo, Jan Vansina, Roland Oliver, and many others.

                    —TREVOR R. GETZ, SERIES EDITOR

Introduction

There are good men [and women] in [the] America[s], but all are very ignorant of Africa. Write down what I tell you exactly as I say it, and be careful to distinguish between what I have seen and what I have only heard other people speak of. They may have made some mistakes; but if you put down exactly what I say, by and by, when good men [and women] go to Africa, they will say, [Lahmen] told the truth.

—Lahmen Kibby (Kebe)

Lahmen Kibby, or Kebe, was captured and exported from his home-land of Futa Jallon sometime in the late eighteenth century. After making an Atlantic crossing, he would spend four decades toiling as an enslaved African in South Carolina, Alabama, and other southern states before receiving his freedom from bondage and a homeward-bound journey (sponsored by the American Colonization Society) in the 1830s. Lahmen's epigraph could be viewed as a departing wish for those in North America—and we would think other parts of the Americas—who only came to know the African through the "magnifi-cent drama" of transatlantic slaving and its associated pejorative images and ideas about Africa, Africans, and African history. Writing a century later about a topic he knew through decades of study rather than experience, the eminent scholar W.E.B. DuBois opined, the "most magnificent drama in the last thousand years of human history is the transportation of ten million human beings out of the dark beauty of their mother continent into the new-found Eldorado of the West."[1] In the spirit of DuBois, this volume introduces readers to Lahmen and a remarkable sample of the millions who experienced this "most

---

[1] W.E.B. DuBois, *Black Reconstruction: An Essay Toward a History of the Part Which Black Folk Played in the Attempt to Reconstruct Democracy in America* (New York: Harcourt, Brace and Co., 1935), 757.

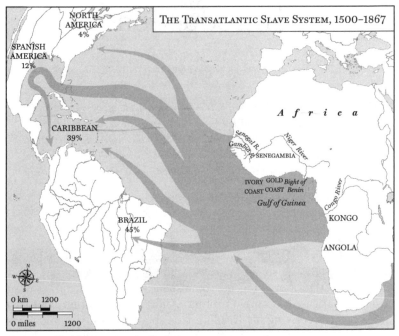

MAP 1 The Transatlantic Slave System, 1500–1867

magnificent drama" in African and world history. In concert with Lahmen's wish, we intend to do so by privileging the voices and perspectives of the enslaved against the hearsay of those who wrote about but did not experience the processes of transatlantic slaving in Africa and in the dispersions and diasporas spawned by it.[2] The overarching purpose of the volume, therefore, is to enlarge the reader's understanding of the internal workings of African societies and their members at various strata in the transatlantic era, strongly emphasize the global context and multiplicity of African experiences during that period, and finally to interpret the process of transatlantic slaving and its consequences through largely African and diasporic primary sources.

---

[2] Our view of transatlantic slaving as a process rather than an institution is also argued in Joseph C. Miller's *The Problem of Slavery as History: A Global Approach* (New Haven, Conn.: Yale University Press, 2012). This view, however, does not mean we subscribe to Miller's central arguments.

THE SOURCES

Historians use a range of sources to craft their narratives about historical times, places, and peoples with whom they did not live, see, or experience. But in this dialogue with the temporally dead, historians are aware such sources have stories of their own, and, at times, the perspectives found in them are at odds with those produced by scholars. The sources used in this study share this quality, which of course poses certain challenges, of which we will limit ourselves to two.

The first challenge for scholars of slaveries involving African (diasporic) peoples concerns which fundamental data best suit the telling of their stories. In 1969, Philip D. Curtin published *The Atlantic Slave Trade: A Census,* which became the first book-length quantitative analysis of the transatlantic slave system. This book remained a foundational source for others and a model they would emulate, as in the Trans-Atlantic Slave Trade Database, first developed in 1999 and enlarged thereafter.[3] Curtin also published an edited text in 1967, *Africa Remembered: Narratives by West Africans from the Era of the Slave Trade,* but such collections or the extensive use of enslaved African narratives in scholarly works are rare. Instead, the quest for "slave trade" statistics and a consequential repression or limited use of African voices has been the tendency.[4] Through a strident resort to

---

[3] The Trans-Atlantic Slave Trade Database is available online at http://www.slavevoyages .org. Based on this database, David Eltis and David Richardson have produced the *Atlas of the Transatlantic Slave Trade* (New Haven, Conn.: Yale University Press, 2010), organized around 189 maps that offer an unprecedented visual account of the transatlantic slave system.

[4] See, for instance, Basil Davidson, *The African Slave Trade* (Boston: Back Bay Books, 1988); Edwards Reynolds, *Stand the Storm: A History of the Atlantic Slave Trade* (Chicago: Elephant Paperbacks, 1993); Lisa A. Lindsay, *Captives as Commodities: The Transatlantic Slave Trade* (Upper Saddle River, N.J.: Pearson, 2008); Joseph E. Inikori and Stanley L. Engerman, eds., *The Atlantic Slave Trade: Effects on Economies, Societies, and Peoples in Africa, the Americas, and Europe* (Durham, N.C.: Duke University Press, 1992); Paul Lovejoy, *Transformations in Slavery: A History of Slavery in Africa* (New York: Cambridge University Press, 2000); Herbert S. Klein, *The Atlantic Slave Trade* (New York: Cambridge University Press, 2010); John K. Thornton, *Africa and Africans in the Making of the Atlantic World, 1400–1800* (New York: Cambridge University Press, 1998); Patrick Manning's *Slavery and African Life: Occidental, Oriental, and African Slave Trades* (New York: Cambridge University Press, 1990); David Northrup, *The Atlantic Slave Trade* (Upper Saddle River, N.J.: Pearson, 1990); James F. Searing, *West African Slavery and Atlantic Commerce: The Senegal River Valley, 1700–1860* (New York: Cambridge

demographic modeling for which little evidence exists or to "slave prices" and trade volume, scholars of captivity in Africa and in its diasporas have chosen nonhuman, abstract data to speak for and thus silence enslaved Africans once more. In effect, we become recipients of the author's perspective in place of the Africans' understandings. We have chosen to respond to this initial challenge by embracing the captives' life stories narrated in Africa and in its Atlantic and western Indian Ocean settings as foundational data in our study. In so doing, we contend that (1) any retelling of transatlantic slaving and its reach into the western Indian Ocean should be anchored in the perspectives of those who experienced an almost endless voyage of (re)capture, kinlessness, and commodification; (2) both African and diasporic narratives of enslavement reveal something critical—in varying quality—about captive and noncaptive life in or after departure from Africa as well as in their host slave societies; and (3) thus these narratives are treated as primary sources laden with histories of rupture, displacement, and eventual estrangement from natal family, community, and from a cultural homeland.

The second challenge concerns the quality or nature of the narrative sources, the specific problems of which has been probed by other historians in some detail.[5] Recently, some have argued that "slave narratives" should be more accurately termed "freedom narratives"

University Press, 1993); Frederick Cooper, *Plantation Slavery on the East Coast of Africa* (New Haven, Conn.: Yale University Press, 1977); Martin A. Klein, *Slavery and Colonial Rule in French West Africa* (New York: Cambridge University Press, 1998); Robert M. Baum, *Shrines of the Slave Trade: Diola Religion and Society in Precolonial Senegambia* (New York: Oxford University Press, 1999); Rosalind Shaw, *Memories of the Slave Trade: Ritual and the Historical Imagination in Sierra Leone* (Chicago: University of Chicago Press, 2002); Walter Hawthorne, *Planting Rice and Harvesting Slaves: Transformations along the Guinea-Bissau Coast, 1400-1900* (Portsmouth, N.H.: Heinemann, 2003).

[5] The problems which "slave narratives" pose are in reality no different than other sources, since each source, as historical evidence, must be placed under the same kinds of scrutiny in terms of the context(es) of its production, who produced it when and for what purpose(s), and the veracity of its content(s). That so-called "slave narratives," originating in North America or in parts of Africa, should pose certain (read: "special") challenges unrelated to any other historical evidence is a case waiting to be demonstrated. For historians who have delved into these matters, see the elaborate discussion for North America in Michael Gomez's *Exchanging Our Country Marks: The Transformation of African Identities in the Colonial and Antebellum South* (Chapel Hill: University of North Carolina Press, 1998), 297-98 n. 12, and, for narratives in Africa, see Pier Larson, "Horrid Journeying: Narrative of Enslavement and the Global African Diaspora," *Journal of World History* 19, no. 4 (2008): 431-64.

when composed or dictated by those born free in Africa, thus distinguishing them from those born into enslavement in the Americas.[6] Given the little "freedom" but the widespread insecurities experienced (including recapture) by the formerly enslaved in and outside of Africa, such an argument seems a bit facile, especially when the central experiences described and the occasion for the composition were—for the vast majority—one of capture, natal alienation, eviction from homeland, and enslavement. In fact, these narratives can also be thought of as texts on early colonialism, where colonialism as a process of alienation from (home) land and labor for the benefit for others was fundamental to transatlantic slaving. But whatever we choose to call those narratives, they do provide details on more than just captivity—hence, their multiple value and use. These sources offer us windows into the lives of captors, captives, returnees, but also the role of commodification, literacy, religious conversion, societal transformation at varying scales, remembrance and representation of earlier lives, and the numerical overrepresentation of Muslims in the total volume of extant narratives though their numbers were much smaller in proportion to the total volume of Africans exported. Lastly, the diverse quality of these sources offers the historian not only an equally diverse set of voices but also functions as a mirror with which to reflect upon the stories of the sources themselves and the perspectives they have to communicate to us. This qualification also applies to the relative strengths and weaknesses of the sources for African societies on the eve of and during the era of transatlantic slaving, since captive life stories with some details about Africa provide underused insights into the internal workings of those societies as well as the host societies where these bonded individuals and families were eventually found.

How these narratives were constructed and under what conditions is as remarkable and dubious as some of the accounts themselves. But readers should know that most, like Lahmen, represented what they experienced, since the recording of one's narrative was an exceptional feat shaped, of course, by the time period(s) and the respective racial ideologies operating in both the Americas and specific parts of Africa.[7] Otherwise, we would have a mountainous set of

---

[6] Paul E. Lovejoy, "'Freedom Narratives' of Transatlantic Slavery," *Slavery & Abolition* 32, no. 1 (2011): 91–107.

[7] For a recent treatment of racial ideology, slavery, and Islam in West Africa operating in the time periods and places to be discussed in this book, see Bruce S. Hall, *A History of Race in Muslim West Africa, 1600–1960* (New York: Cambridge University Press, 2011), 4, 13–15, and especially chapters 1 and 2.

captive accounts able to fill the stacks of several major libraries. The opportunity for literary self-representation required in most cases some competence in the writing and speaking of European languages or a European/white person competent in Arabic and, in rare cases, an African language. Though many enslaved Africans were multilingual, they remain without a documentary voice because language alone was insufficient. Gaining a modicum of freedom from bondage and acquiring the patronage of sympathetic European/white holders, missionaries, abolitionists, or amanuenses (persons to whom an account is dictated) usually made the narrative process feasible. But, here, the variable of language had its own trappings: the idioms, syntax, and "gendered" nature of the source (European) languages codified realities for which such languages could not amicably describe or explain as conceived in the minds and speech of the African (multilingual) speaker. Thus, for instance, readers should use guided caution when they encounter the narrator's use of racial classifications or the fervent use of the terms "nations" or "country" when describing their or another's homeland or cultural group. Enslaved Africans rarely demarcated "ethnic" differences, as present-day writers have claimed and even reified in the literature. Instead, many commented on socio-cultural practices and speech patterns as markers of distinction and overlap. Once individuals were able to adequately dictate or compose in a language and have it published (usually through some kind of sponsorship or subscription), internal issues about the composition itself still remained. Abolitionists and missionaries of various stripes, for instance, encouraged the recording of life experiences as part of their propaganda; where these purposes were less than explicit, such autobiographies often followed certain templates, ensuring conformity and utility for each cause and their audiences. But what is remarkable about many of the accounts the reader will find herein is that, in spite of these strictures, the gravitational force of memory and the concern for kin and community in a cultural homeland or in a host slave society shines through the cloud of propaganda. Viewed against the foregoing arguments, scholars who write about and students who study these matters need not be held captive to the very means for our insights—the sources.

FRAMING TRANSATLANTIC SLAVING

Transatlantic slaving occupied a fairly straightforward chronology—from the mid-fifteenth to the end of the nineteenth century—but its (unwilling) participants and unfolding processes varied, being at times extremely disorganized while in other instances agile and sophisticated. Moreover, a common view of African societies on the eve of transatlantic slaving is that such societies were anthropologically "primitive" and without social complexity because, it was thought, they lacked the tools, arms, and innovations of European civilizations. Against this deficiency thesis, undifferentiated Africans "sold" their own and "ethnic" rivals for metals, guns, textiles, and symbolic items that conferred status in the recipient's society. Recent archaeological research into the deep history of African societies paints a different yet composite picture of complex social orders as diverse as Africa's ecologies. These societies were characterized by ample interactions and interdependencies between farmers, foragers, pastoralists, and fishers living in or on the frontier of settlements and states varying in size and egalitarianism and where most placed greater emphasis on wealth in people rather than in products. Historians of Africa have helped to fill these generic categories of human action and historical processes with the metaphorical soft tissue of lived experiences—for a range of individuals and some communities better than others. The sheer range of settlements and socio-political complexities casts great doubt on the received wisdom above, and between the archaeologist's shovel and the historian's devotion to documents, we now know that transatlantic slaving was less than systematic but developed along specific geographies and in relation to specific societies, which came disproportionately under its spell. A chronological and spatial framework is thus needed to put these specificities into perspective and to chart the growth of transatlantic slaving rather than assume its maturity or the underdevelopment of African societies in their encounters with Atlantic commerce.

By the early thirteenth century, Genoese and Venetian merchants had already established slaving ports using captive "Slavs," among others, to produce sugar for export within a trade system that stretched from the Atlantic, through the Mediterranean, to the Black Sea. On the Atlantic end of this network the Iberian nations of Portugal and Spain were aided by the Italian model of plantation slavery and soon extended this system to islands off and in specific locales on the mainland of northwest to west central Africa by the sixteenth century. In the previous century, the "Slavs" and other captives were being increasingly replaced by African ones brought to Portugal, Spain, and France, in part fed by Portuguese slaving voyages as well as Arab-Muslim slaving across the Sahara and through North African ports in

Morocco, Tunisia, and Libya. Thus, the African source for peopling the Americas in early transatlantic slaving was not Africa per se, but rather captive and "Iberianized" Africans from Spain and Portugal. As part of the *Reconquista*, the Christian retaking of the Iberian Peninsula from Islamic control, the Portuguese expelled their Muslim overloads, acquired some essential nautical knowledge and technologies through Muslim scholars (who obtained their know-how from as far as China), added the cannon to their vessels, and established plantations off the coast of western Africa while raiding Africans communities for captives. Raiding would partially give way to commercial relations—cemented by gifts, fraud, military force, and baptisms—and Portugal and Spain would dominate the transatlantic slave system until the mid-seventeenth century. Dutch, Danish, Swedish, French, and Brandenburger (German) trafficking notwithstanding, England would dominate the north Atlantic and Portugal the south Atlantic commerce until the first decade of the nineteenth century for the former and the end of that century for the latter. By then, transatlantic slaving had already extended itself in the western Indian Ocean, beginning as early as the mid-eighteenth century. It is not surprising then by whom and how transatlantic slaving developed: geographically from northern Senegambia to Sierra Leone to the Gulf of Guinea to west central Africa and southeast Africa, and temporally from the mid-fifteenth century to the end of the nineteenth century. In sum, it is more accurate to think spatially of transatlantic slaving less as a triangle with Africa, the Americas, and Europe at each endpoint but rather as a hexagon illustrating the multidirectional roots and routes of the six major slaving zones: Europe; West Africa; West Central Africa; Southeast Africa; the South Atlantic facing South America; and the North Atlantic facing the Caribbean and North America.

OUTLINE OF THE CHAPTERS

Our spatial-chronological framework guides the structure of each chapter, emphasizing commonalties and variation at the scale of regions, localities, and individuals so that readers can follow their stories and make spatial, historical, and thematic connections at once. By placing African experiences in global and local contexts, we highlight the ways in which Africans were brought under, shaped by, and in turn influenced the course of the transatlantic slave system. We also break from the paradigm of silencing African voices—voices concerned deeply with matters of kin and community—and thus privilege a diverse set of African accounts in the retelling of the transatlantic story. To be clear, this volume is not a study in (auto)biography or a densely annotated selection of such source materials. But we do put (auto)biographies to use—and have purposely limited our footnoting to essential citations—in order to communicate a story larger than individual biographies. By so doing, we have organized the volume into four chapters and an epilogue, built around specific sources and narratives that are themselves linked to wider issues in African and world history. On the whole, the chapters consider the mechanisms of enslavement, the socio-political and cultural context from which captives and captors were drawn, the global flow of capital and captive Africans, and African understandings of the transatlantic slave system in Africa and its diasporas. Although the chapters are analytically linked to the theme of retelling the story of the transatlantic slave system through African understandings, the order in which they can be read is flexible, so that instructors, for instance, can assign the chapters in the order best suited for their course.

The first chapter, The Anchors: African Understandings of Their Societies and "Slavery," focuses on a broad network of ideas linked to social ordering and strata, categories of "free" and servile labor, and their changing meanings across distinct and overlapping African landscapes during the late fifteenth century and the early nineteenth century. Within this survey, the chapter has two related goals. First, it explores how notions of what we call "slavery" and "slaves" were understood or not by Africans in their own times and through their own experiences. Here, the available life stories of enslaved Africans are used to examine notions of society and the place of "slavery" in it, thus providing "anchors" for the chapters to follow. Second, the chapter engages readers in a re-evaluation of familiar assumptions and related key questions, which all underscore why we should use the term "slavery" with guided caution, since categories of servile labor and status, as well as their changing meaning over time, must be distinguished rather than lumped under the rubric of "African slavery" or under the idea that Africans were "selling" each other before European contact and so the latter simply tapped into an existing system of enslavement. In this way, as the chapter argues, we further clarify the relationship between local forms of captivity and servitude and the global demands of the transatlantic slave system while excavating the African perspectives at the intersection of both.

The second chapter, Vessels and Villains: African Understandings of Atlantic Commerce and Commodification, picks up where the previous ended by examining various African systems of commerce and their local, regional, and even transnational character, and how these experiences prepared Africans for or departed from the dynamics of Atlantic commerce and commodification. It is important to grapple with African understandings of commodification, since commodification of African humanity was deeply crucial to transatlantic slaving and represented new forms of dehumanization and homogenization—where a multitude of peoples were smashed into new identities as "Negroes" or "Africans" or "Igbos"—at a time when most African societies valued people above property and goods and when most European merchants were accepting "payment" almost exclusively in humans. In the transformation of Africans into captives and then commodities and laboring chattel, the villains were manifold, as were the vessels or the modes of transport within and from homelands to a diaspora and from individuals who could write their own destinies to ones with subjugated fates. This state of affairs also meant that a number of African states became more stratified and local communities commodified, so much so that a number of decentralized peoples were transformed into slave-trading communities. African understandings of these transformations are central to wider concerns of Atlantic human trafficking and commodification within the entangled histories of Europe, Africa, and the Americas.

The third chapter, Black Bodies at Bay and Reversing Sail: African Understandings of Self, Religion, and Returning Home, has a twofold purpose, which is reflected in its structure. In the first half, we draw attention to African understandings of identity during the transatlantic era in contrast to two views: those of European onlookers, who principally interpreted matters of sexuality, gender, and cultural identity through their own religious and cultural lens, and those of "Europeanized" Africans who sought to refashion themselves, in part or in whole, in terms of "European" conceptions of the aforementioned. These understandings, as articulated through African narratives of enslavement, will help locate the reader in the socio-cultural worlds of the African as to the meaning or usefulness of the above notions and the limitations of reading back in time current preoccupations with cultural identity and gender. Rather than view notions of gender, sexuality, and cultural identity as ontological givens, they will be treated as theoretical tools to be tested against the lived experiences of enslaved Africans during the transatlantic era. The second half of this chapter explores transatlantic slaving as an uneven set of religious encounters and contestations between or among Christian, Islamic, and indigenous African spiritual adherents. African understandings of these important historical processes—and a resistance to them—are critical, since those "liberated" Africans who returned to nineteenth-century Africa did so largely as Christianized individuals and proselytes for an "Africa" different from the one they or their ancestors left.

The fourth chapter, The Endless Voyage of Cannibalism and Capitalism: African Understandings of the Impacts of Transatlantic Slaving and Abolitionism, weighs the central arguments of the previous chapters through the lens of African metaphors and cultural idioms in the nineteenth century, so as to offer a composite view of the ways in which Africans grappled with and are still, in many ways, interpreting the impact of transatlantic slaving on self, society, and the diasporas spawned by it. This chapter, like the previous ones, privileges enslaved African rather than scholarly interpretations—of which there are plenty. Such African interpretations are essential to a fuller understanding of the transatlantic slave system and its human consequences. To be sure, African readings of that system as an endless voyage of cannibalism and capitalism were widespread among the published voices and the voiceless. These widespread beliefs of cannibalism among Africans from Senegambia to Southeast Africa were matched by similar beliefs among European and Arab-Muslim slavers who, through their religious lenses, remained convinced that Africans were cannibals and pagans. In the Americas, white soldiers, planters, and politicians willfully accepted that "these poor pagans and (in many cases) cannibals from the coast of Africa" would only "cease to be cannibals and savages" by "Christian civilization" in ways akin to the "domestication of wild animals and fowls." The Africans' presumed cannibalism and paganism was calcified as a fixed truth during the transatlantic era and reified as the foremost character of "black" labor forces in colonial and postcolonial contexts.

In the epilogue, Almost Home: Forgetful Memories and Getting the Stories Right, we remind readers that slavery did not end with the imposition of laws and through the actions of naval squadrons, nor did abolition put an end to servitude. Manumission did not miraculously cure the damage done by enslavement. Emancipation was not a panacea for the ills caused by the slaving system. Nor can the slavery of the past be neatly packaged into an official or academic "history" and then placed to the side as if it does not have any legacy in the minds of individuals, the collective memories of societies, and the organization of communities and states today. For that reason, we chose to close this book not with a conclusion that "ends" the story, but rather with an exploration of the ways in which the Atlantic slaving system continues to resonate and affect us today. This is not an exploration of where slavery still exists today, although it is clear that the experiences of enslavement are still to be found on some rural plantations and in some urban households. Rather, we want to continue to focus on the massive forced migration of the Atlantic slaving system by looking at the ways in which it is still known, understood, and dealt with in popular culture on both sides of the Atlantic. We will ask three important questions: How do Atlantic societies and especially diasporic and continental African societies choose to remember the Atlantic slaving system today? What are the contests and debates about how that past should be remembered, or alternately forgotten, and what do they tell us about our own society? Finally, what should the relationship be between works of history like this book and popular memories of the Atlantic slaving system? For the historian, the study of memory is thus an essential part of our ever-present labors to get the stories right, especially for those historically silenced, and to fight against the common bacteria of forgetting those who should be remembered.

The Anchors: African Understandings of Their Societies and "Slavery"

I do not know my family, for enemies carried me off when I was still a child. . . .
Woe is me that I have no relations.

—Chisi Ndjurisiye Sichyajunga

How do we arrive at African understandings of their societies and approach the processes and forms of servitude therein? Through the experiences of captives and through the lens of family, of course, Chisi Sichyajunga would have argued. Chisi was born sometime in the 1870s and related her story of capture, captivity, and escape in early twentieth-century Central Africa. In relating her account, Chisi invoked not abstract notions of freedom but rather the ideas of belonging and familial bonds that resonated deeply in the lives of so many before her. Though her life story was recorded during the first decades of European colonial rule and at a time when legal forms of enslavement had but all disappeared, Chisi began her narrative like the vast majority of enslaved individuals who left a documentary trail in Africa and its worldwide diaspora, focusing on the ubiquitous twin themes of family and natal community. Why family and community? Should we interpret these terms as two faces of the same coinage? Yes and no. Yes, we can, but there is, in spite of obvious synergy between the two, a distinction to be made. Communities are constellations of families and strangers who need not possess a shared bloodline or ideology, whereas individuals are either born or incorporated (after a few generations and through reproduction) into a family and thus assume specific identities, bonds, and obligations that can remain regardless of which communities such individuals decide to join. In effect, family and the layers of relationships to temporal and spiritual members thereof exercised a tremendous weight on the self-understandings of individuals and on the societies in which they were found or kept as captive or "free" members. The origins and ordering of many African societies boiled down to the sociopolitical arrangements of first-arrival families or migrant families to a locality, the divisions of power and labor established among them and those incorporated as newcomers, the social dependencies within and between communities or states, and the relationships and conflicts arising out of these processes, leading eventually to the capture and removal of individuals like Chisi from their natal homeland and family. In the end, capture and enslavement represented what it meant to be kinless ("I have no relations"), and transitory or sustained freedom from either capture or enslavement entailed the reconstitution of kinship bonds – wherever and with captors or fellow captives.

Rather than assume transatlantic slaving was simply a transactional matter between captives and captors or that "Atlantic Africa" was the only region shaped by this international process, this chapter focuses on a broad network of ideas linked to social ordering and strata, categories of "free" and servile labor, and their changing meanings across distinct and overlapping African landscapes from the late fifteenth through the early nineteenth century. Within this survey, the chapter has two related goals. First, it will explore how notions of what we call "slavery" and "slaves" were understood or not by Africans in their own times and through their own experiences. Here, the available life stories of enslaved Africans will be used to examine notions of society and the place of "slavery" in it, thus providing "anchors" for the chapters to follow. Second, the chapter will engage readers in a reevaluation of familiar assumptions and related key questions. In much of the scholarship, "slavery" is an institution that often presupposes

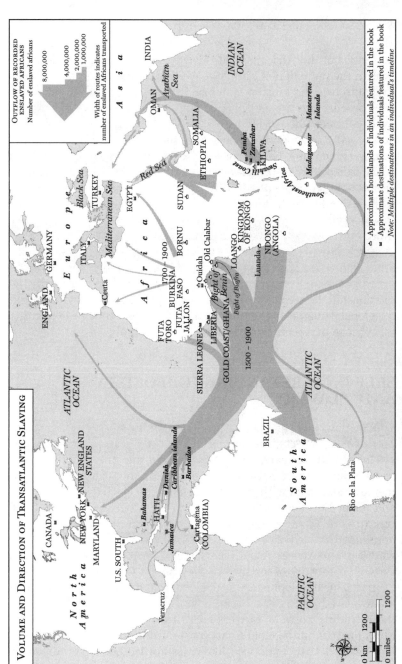

MAP 2 Volume and Direction of Transatlantic Slaving

VOLUME AND DIRECTION OF TRANSATLANTIC SLAVING

OUTFLOW OF RECORDED ENSLAVED AFRICANS
Number of enslaved africans

8,000,000
4,000,000
2,000,000
1,000,000

Width of routes indicates number of enslaved Africans transported

⚑ Approximate homelands of individuals featured in the book
■ Approximate destinations of individuals featured in the book
Note: Multiple destinations in an individual's timeline

3

captivity, but did Africans hold this view? If they did, how does one explain the reduction of kinfolk to captives or the absorption of captives into existing kinship systems? In many African contexts, captives procured as a result of war, famine, raid, kidnapping, or debt were political and social assets and individuals to be acquired, exchanged, and absorbed because they had cash, labor, tributary, and demographic value. Numerous captives were also assimilated after a generation or two into local society, while some never fully integrated because of the stigma of a "captive" past. These processes underscore why we should use the term "slavery" with guided caution, for categories of servile labor and status, as well as their changing meaning over time, must be delineated rather than lumped under the rubric of "African slavery" or under the idea that Africans were "selling" each other before European contact and so the latter simply tapped into an existing system of enslavement. In this way we will further clarify the relationship between local forms of captivity and servitude and the global demands of the transatlantic slave system while excavating the African perspectives at the intersection of both.

SELF-UNDERSTANDINGS OF SOCIETY AND "SLAVERY"

This section explores Africans' understandings of their societies and processes of "slavery," beginning in the early years of transatlantic slaving. In those years, West African gold and the conduit of the trans-Saharan trade network began to give way to an Atlantic commerce preoccupied with gold and then human exports, first to Iberia and major European cities and then to the Americas. The Mediterranean world waned as a zone of commercial importance, and Portugal dominated the export flow of gold and captives from northwest to west central Africa, including islands like Arguin and Madeira, through a network of fortified trading posts (*feitorias*) under crown control. This development was of global importance since it signaled a new era of Portuguese overseas and colonial expansion. Some of those trading posts or fortress-factories, such as the São Jorge da Mina fortress on the Gold Coast (present-day Ghana), became colonial enclaves that functioned like cities nestled between indigenous communities and the authority of the Portuguese empire. In fact, Portuguese officials at the Mina fortress and in Lisbon often referred to São Jorge da Mina as "our city," and as this fortress became their base of operation in West Africa by the late fifteenth century, the substantial commerce in gold and captives meant that rules that governed enslavement and freedom in Lisbon also applied to the colonial outposts.[1] A rare 1499 manumission letter which legally freed a formerly enslaved woman named Beatriz Gomes on the Gold Coast puts these matters into clearer focus, offering insight into the limits of what we can and cannot know about the early ebb and flow of transatlantic slaving and of the voices of those drowned out its in currents. The manumission was made by Pedro Goncalves, resident of the Island of Madeira. He had purchased Beatriz in the Mina fortress during a recent trip there. It would appear that he had either resided at the fortress for a time or was one of the ship suppliers to the fortress. The manumission was given in Lisbon on April 16, 1499, but the transaction was approved by the commander (*capitão mor*) of the Mina fortress on April 20, with the final portion of the manumission letter asserting proper payments had been made and that an inquiry into the religious conversion requirements for Beatriz had been met. This final part was dated the first of May, presumably upon the closing of the manumission process.[2]

There was, however, nothing about the origin or condition of Beatriz's enslavement or anything else by or about her. Beyond the general pursuit of gold, liquor, and women of African-Portuguese parentage, Portuguese officials and fort personnel at São Jorge da Mina were more concerned with inventory than the identity of enslaved individuals like Beatriz. The enslaved, like all trade goods, could be liquidated with only the vaguest of notation in the surviving records. We know Beatriz was sold at the Mina fortress, but where did she come from, and was Beatriz her birth name? We know she was manumitted, but on what grounds? We know from indigenous Gold Coast women like Graça and Adwoa that indigenous names were recorded (as in the case of the latter) and there were tensions between local spiritualities and Catholicism, but we do not know if either was true

---

[1] On São Jorge da Mina and the trade between Portugal and the Gold Coast, see John Vogt, *Portuguese Rule on the Gold Coast, 1469–1682* (Athens: University of Georgia Press, 1979); Ivana Elbl, *The Portuguese Trade with West Africa, 1440–1521* (Ph.D. dissertation, University of Toronto, 1986); John W. Blake, *Europeans in West Africa, 1450–1560* (London: The Hakluyt Society, 1942); Christopher R. DeCorse, *An Archaeology of Elmina: Africans and Europeans on the Gold Coast, 1400–1900* (Washington, D.C.: Smithsonian Institution Press, 2001).

[2] Instituto dos Arquivos Nacionais/Torre do Tombo (IAN/TT), Chancelaria de D. Manuel I, liv. 16, fl. 45v.

for Beatriz.[3] We also know that Beatriz, at least to the authorities, professed to be a Catholic, but did she discard her indigenous spiritual practices and ideas or did she combine options provided by the two? The above and so many other important questions must yield to the design of the document – it was meant to record a legal transaction – and unless further records are discovered, we will never know much about the interior lives and the local societies from which early transatlantic captives such as Beatriz came. From the sixteenth-century western Sudan, which the Portuguese first brought into the transatlantic commercial orbit and where enslavement and Islam co-existed, we know something of the social orders where captive peoples were found—from such locally produced sources as the *Tarikh al-fattash* ("Chronicle of the researcher") by Ibn al-Mukhtar—but comparatively almost nothing about those bonded individuals.[4]

The following excerpts from the *Tarikh al-fattash* reveals the widespread but distinct forms of captivity and servitude—and the distribution of power and wealth—in the territorially vast Songhay Empire but also the anonymity of the enslaved:

In each of the villages situated in the lands that we have listed, without a single exception, the prince had slaves and a *fanfa*. Under the orders of certain of his *fanfa* were found 100 slaves employed in the cultivation of the soil; while in others there were only 60, 50, 40 or 20. The word *fanfa*, which is *fanafi* in the plural, designates a chief of slaves, but it is also used to designate the owner of a boat.

[T]his prince owned . . . [a] plantation was occupied by 200 slaves with 4 *fanfa*, who were placed under the orders of a chief called Missakoulallah. . . . The custom was that, only the *askia* [ruler of Songhay] provided the seed destined for that plantation as well as the hides that were used to make the *sounnou* [a unit of measure]. The boats used to transport that product to the residence of the *askia*

---

[3] For Graça, see IAN/TT, Tribunal do Santo Ofício, Inquisição de Lisboa, proc. 11041 [ca. 1540]; for Adwoa, who is named Maria in the document, see A. Teixeira da Mota and P.E.H. Hair, *East of Mina: Afro-European Relations on the Gold Coast in the 1550s and 1560s: An Essay with Supporting Documents* (Madison: University of Wisconsin–Madison, 1988), 75.

[4] On slavery and Islam in African (diaspora) contexts, see Chouki El Hamel, *Black Morocco: A History of Slavery, Race and Islam* (New York: Cambridge University Press, 2013); Paul Lovejoy, ed., *Slavery on the Frontiers of Islam* (Princeton, N.J.: Markus Wiener, 2004); John Hunwick and Eve Troutt Powell, *The African Diaspora in the Mediterranean Lands of Islam* (Princeton, N.J.: Markus Wiener, 2002); Ronald Segal, *Islam's Black Slaves: The Other Black Diaspora* (New York : Farrar, Straus and Giroux, 2001); John Ralph Willis, *Slaves and Slavery in Muslim Africa*, 2 vols. (London: F. Cass, 1985).

numbered 10. By the envoy charged with placing the harvest in the *sounnou*, the *askia* sent 1000 *gouro* [kola] nuts to the chief of the *fanfa*, a whole salt bar and a black *boubou* [an item of clothing], also a great cloth for the wife of that chief: this was the custom fixed by the *askia*, as well as his successor. When the day came, the *fanfa* sent to tell their chief Missakoulallah that the moment had come to gather the harvest, which was ripe, but they would not lay a hand on the sickle until he came himself and see the field, he went out for three days and did a tour of all four sides, and once he returned, gave them the order to make the harvest.

A certain year, the envoys of the *fanfa* having arrived to advise him that the grain was ripe and ready to harvest, he took his canoe, according to the custom, with his drums and his followers; arriving at the plantation, he saw that the grain was ripe and spent about three days touring the field. Then he went to a village near the plantation called Denki Doumde and sailed to the port of that place. Then he sent for the *imam* of the village, the students, the poor and the widows, as soon as they arrived, he said to them, "Who has the right to the product of this plantation?" "Who then," they replied to him, "would have rights beyond the owner, that is, the *askia*?" "It is I," replied Missakoulallah, who personally has the right for this year and I would like to make an offering which will profit me in the other world and make me right with God. I will make an offering to you for the love of God; cut and harvest that field: that for the poor and unfortunate among you who are not able to obtain canoes reaped the first heads of grain that fall from your sickles, to the owners of the great canoes give the center of the field. God will agree on this offering of mine!" He returned then to his village and gave a present to each of the *fanfa*, from what he possessed himself, from a field that provided for his subsistence.[5]

At first glance, the above passages strongly suggest a hierarchical ordering of settlements under the management of an empire that stretched from the Atlantic coast to Kano north of the tropical rain forest—and thus savanna and Sahel lands—but interspersed with highlands and plateaus and the Senegal, Gambia, and Niger rivers. But at second glance, we see interlocking but not necessarily vertical levels of subservience, power, and wealth, wherein some of the enslaved plantation workers, including the "overseers" or *fanafi*, were very wealthy, and they too held or managed captive peoples. The *fanafi*, in turn, were "placed under the orders of a chief called Missakoulallah," who served the "prince" and who served or followed the dictates of the "owner" of the land and the provider of the seed – the

---

5 Ibn al-Mukhtar, *Tarikh al-Fettash fi akhbar al-buldan wa 'l-juyush wa-akabir al-nas*, eds. and trans. Octave Houdas and Maurice Delafosse (Paris: Adrien-Maisonneuve, 1913–14 [1964]), 179–81 (italics added).

askia. Among these relations of power and people on the one hand and between common peoples, their labor, and the land on the other are the nuances of social relationships and a social order maintained by interdependencies. The *fanfa* was not simply an estate manager, an overseer, an owner of the boat used to transport crops, or a likely captive person himself—he was all the above. But his loyalty, and the sense of belonging and identification created among those ranking above and below him, was facilitated by "offerings" and "presents" made by the *fanfa* leader, Missakoulallah, to each *fanfa*, and, likewise, the *askia*'s offering of valuable commodities in cloth, salt, and kola nuts to Missakoulallah only lubricated the joints on which the empire was structured. And in that structure, as the source demonstrates, the poor, the student, the widow, and the unfortunate had a place, and they too reaped from the harvest, for the web of sociopolitical relations, however exploitative, provided all a sense of security and belonging built on kinship networks.

Though the *Tarikh al-fattash* excerpts provide a sixteenth-century (and in some cases a seventeenth-century) view of social ordering in the western Sudanic region, and though its insights into social relations applies to other parts of Africa, it by no means offers a panoramic view of the continent as seen by its indigenous and especially its servile populations. And though it is partially accurate that "precolonial" African history lacks extensive primary sources produced by Africans themselves, the early documented history for two major slaving regions in west central Africa—the Kingdom of Kôngo and that of Ndongo (Angola)—offer additional insights in African social ordering, although the voices come from state leaders who protected their own families, while sanctioning the seizure and eviction of "other" citizens during the early transatlantic era. As was true for the western Sudan as recorded in the *Tarikh al-fattash* and the Gold Coast and its political neighbors, the Kingdom of Kôngo owes its origins to the very kinship structures found elsewhere in Africa. In fact, the early origins of Kôngo date to the mid- to late fourteenth century, when ambitious and conquering male rulers used marriage alliances to ensure that political succession would flow from them to their children and to bind a number of polities north and south of the Kôngo River, and extending to the coast, to the impending Kôngo state. Soon the Kôngo state overshadowed those allied and smaller polities, who would come to recognize the ruler of Kôngo but without relinquishing control over their own domains. Meanwhile, Kôngo expanded further, conquered and integrated new polities as provinces ruled by member of the nobility, and forced those under its rule to pay a tribute.[6] It was this Kingdom of Kôngo under the rule of *manikongo* ("ruler") Nzinga Nkuwu (baptized in 1491 as João I) that received the Portuguese in the late fifteenth century.

What we know about the Kingdom of Kôngo during the first half of the sixteenth century comes from the voluminous letters of Nzinga Mbemba (baptized Afonso I; ruler of Kôngo, ca. 1509–42), the son of Nzinga Nkuwu and the first and most reputed promoter of Christianity and Europeanization in the Kôngo. Once the governor of the Nsundi province in northeastern Kôngo, Mbemba ascended the throne with Portuguese support after the death of his father in 1509 and amidst much opposition from his half-brother Mpanzu a Kitima; in a word, "all the people and relatives and brothers were against us."[7] In fact, Mbemba's father viewed him and his Christian kin with acute cynicism, wanting "Dom Pedro [Mbemba's Christian cousin] brought to his compound where he would order him to be killed to see whether [his Christian] God would deliver him from there; and the king [Nzinga a Nkuwu] said that he would take away our incomes and would leave us to wander about like men blown by the wind until we died, or until he ordered us killed."[8] Against this wave of opposition but with Portuguese armed support, Mbemba ascended to the throne of Kôngo. The following passages, excerpted from Mbemba's letters, speak to a watershed moment in the history of Kôngo—the beginnings of its undoing—set in the transatlantic era. In a letter to Manuel I, king of Portugal (October 5, 1514), Mbemba or his clerk wrote the following:

> [After the arrival of some Portuguese priests . . .] we gave them [money] so that they all began to deal in buying and selling. We [told them . . .] if they were to buy some slaves, they should not purchase any women. . . . Yet notwithstanding they began to fill the houses with whores, in such a fashion that Father Pero Fernandes impregnated a woman in his house and she gave birth to a mulatto.
> . . . [W]e sent a letter to your Highness and another to Queen Dona Leonor – and with our relatives we sent 700 manilhas, many slaves, parrots, animals, and civet cats. . . . [E]ach of them [masons] already had bought from 15 to 20 slaves. . . . Those masons left, and took as many slaves and goods as they had, and no more

---

[6] John Thornton, "The Origins and Early History of the Kingdom of Kongo, c. 1350–1550," *The International Journal of African Historical Studies* 34, no. 1 (2001): 89–120; Linda M. Heywood, "Slavery and Its Transformation in the Kingdom of Kongo, 1491–1800," *Journal of African History* 50 (2009): 1–22.

[7] Antonio Brasio, ed., *Monumenta Missionaria Africana*, 1st Ser. 15 vols. (Lisbon: Ageência Geral do Ultramar, 1952–88), 1: 295–317. Hereafter, *MMA*.

[8] *MMA*, 1: 294–95.

than three remained here. We dispatched the said ship promptly and sent 200 manilhas and 60 slaves to Fernão de Melo, aside from those we gave to his servants; and we sent our nephew Pedro Afonso on the ship, with a letter to your highness in which we gave an account of affairs here, and sent your Highness 200 manilhas and certain slaves, so that Pedro Afonso could take them to Portugal and buy us some clothes there. . . . [In] the large ship and the caravel we sent two of our nephews, with our son Dom Francisco – and 500 slaves for both ships, with 30 extra slaves, so that if some of the 500 slaves died their number could be made up from the 30.

. . . And Dom Pedro took 190 slaves – that is 100 of ours and 90 for your Highness – to make up for those who had remained here because they were too thin. With him went all our nephews, and he was to convey our obedience to the Pope. . . . Some priests come . . . and they all began to buy slaves – in spite of the fact that Your Highness' instructions forbade it. And then we posted our own decree that no one was to buy slaves except the factor. . . .[9]

Mbemba penned, "We were ready to suffer for the love our Lord God," and, indeed, the Kôngo did suffer. In another letter to João III (July 6, 1526), Mbemba complained about the Portuguese priests and merchants he invited and how their voracious greed had besieged the Kôngo:

. . . Your Highness should know how our Kingdom is being lost in so many ways that it is convenient to provide for the necessary remedy, since this is caused by the excessive freedom given by your factors and officials to the men and merchants who are allowed to come to this Kingdom and set up shops with goods and many things which have been prohibited by us. . . . And we cannot reckon how great the damage is, since the mentioned merchants are taking every day our natives, sons of the land and the sons of our noblemen and vassals and our relatives, because the thieves and men of bad conscience grab them wishing to have the things and wares of this Kingdom which they are ambitious of; they grab them and get them to be sold; and so great, sir is the corruption and licentiousness that our country is being completely depopulated. . . . [I]t is our will that in these kingdoms there should not be any trade of slaves or outlet for them.[10]

In October of 1526, Mbemba again writes to João III, complaining of the ways in which imported European goods created a predatory environment among his people:

. . . Moreover, in our kingdoms there is another great inconvenience which is of little service to God, and this is that many of our people, keenly desirous as they are of the wares and things of your kingdoms, which are brought her by your people, and in order to satisfy their voracious appetite, seize many of our people, freed and exempt men; and very often it happens that they kidnap nobleman and the sons of noblemen, and our relatives, and take them to be sold to the white men who are in our kingdoms; and for this purpose they have concealed them; and others are brought during the night so that they might not be recognized.[11]

And as soon as they are taken by the white men they are immediately ironed and branded with fire, and when they are carried to be embarked. . . .

And to avoid such a great evil we passed a law so that any white man living in our Kingdoms and wanting to purchase goods in any way should first inform three of our noblemen and officials of our court whom we rely upon in this matter . . . if cleared by them [the appointed noblemen and officials] there will be no further doubt nor embargo for them to be taken and embarked. But if the white men do not comply with it they will lose the aforementioned goods [i.e., enslaved peoples]. And if we do them this favor and concession it is for the part Your Highness has in it, since we know that it is in your service too that these goods are taken from our kingdom. . . .

Judging from these letters, the internal decline of an independent Kôngo began during Mbemba's reign and in the warring factions seeking the throne thereafter. This all came to head when Kôngo–Portuguese relations took a turn for the worse with the Portuguese invasion of Angola in the 1620s and the crippling civil wars (ca. 1665–1709) after the death of anti-Portuguese ruler Garcia II (r. 1641–61), prompting more internal squabbling. It is with the invasion of Angola that Njinga Mbande of Ndongo and Matamba came into political picture. Born around 1582 in the Kingdom of Ndongo, Njinga was the eldest child of the kingdom's ruler, Mbandi Ngola—"Ngola" became the source of the territory called "Angola." In the Kingdom of Kôngo where political power was male-dominated, Kôngo women of noble stature exercised some power, but symbolically and through their roles as lineage heads and as mothers of key male political figures. Though some Kôngo women would come to exercise considerable political power after the period of civil war, none became rulers of the kingdom, as was the case in the Kingdom of Ndongo, starting with Njinga. After claiming the throne in the wake of her brother's suicide in 1624, Njinga, like Mbemba, was also Christianized (baptized as Ana de Sousa) and engaged in the process of transatlantic slaving. In an early letter (March 3, 1625) to the Portuguese commander in eastern Angola, Njinga or her scribe wrote:

. . . I will give you an account of how as I was sending some slaves to the market of Bumba Aquiçanzo, Aire came out with his army, and robbed me of thirty slaves of

---

[11] *MMA* 1: 489.

those I had sent I sought satisfaction against my vassal my army met with nine men who were with the Tiger [a Portuguese field commander] in the land, and putting upon these nine who went to meet my army outside of Pedra [a fortress] it pleased God that they were defeated by mine where I brought back six alive. . . . Your Grace, send me a hair net and four yards of gram for a cover, and a bedspread of montaria, and good wine, and a arroba of wax from Vellas, and a half dozen Indian colored cloths and two or three table cloths of Rendas, some red, blue and wine-colored rubies, and a sun hat of blue velvet, or the one that you wear, and 100 folios of paper.[12]

In another letter (December 13, 1655) to the Governor General of Angola, Njinga wrote, in the context of peace treaty negotiations beginning in 1626 with the Portuguese,

I have complained so much to the past governors, who have always promised to return my sister [captured by the Portuguese in battle], to which end I have given infinite slaves and done thousands of *banzos* [trading goods], and she was never returned but after wars were made to disquiet me and make me always go about as Jaga [Imbangala; fierce warriors used as mercenaries by Njinga and the Portuguese], using tyrannies, some as not allowing children, this being the style of *quilombo* [military encampment], and other ceremonies, with I have completely given up. . . .

. . . Concerning the two hundred slaves which Your Lordship asks for the ransom of my sister D. Barbora [Kijunji], it is a very rigorous price, I have given the slaves which Your Lordship already must know, to past governors and ambassadors, outside mimos and secretaries and servants of your house, and many residents, that already today I feel tricked. That which our Lordship wishes me to give would be 130 slaves, the 100 I will send when my sister [is] in Embaca [Mbaka, a town and fort belonging to the Portuguese colony of Angola, and a point through most captives from the deep interior left their homelands via Luanda]. . . .[13]

Near the end of her life, Njinga wrote a letter (June 15, 1660) to Antonio de Oliveira de Cadornega, resident historian and slave dealer in Angola, about runaway captives and responded to the claim that she harbored them:

---

[12] Queen Njinga to Bento Banha Cardoso, 3 March 1625, quoted in Fernão de Sousa to Gonçalo de Sousa and his brothers (ca. 1630), in Beatrix Heintze, ed., *Fontes para a história de Angola do século XVII.*, 2 vols. (Wiesbaden, Germany, 1985–88) 1: 244–45.

[13] *MMA*, 11: 524–28. On Mbaka and how transatlantic slaving adversely affected this society at the level of villages and households, see Jan Vansina, "Ambaca Society and the Slave Trade, c. 1760–1845," *Journal of African History* 46 (2005): 1–27.

The letter which your grace wrote to me concerning your runaway people which my people sold or stole, this is said by people who wish ill to the peace and Christianity, because if your grace could ask all the Pumbeiros [agents dispatched by merchants to acquired inland captives] of the whites who come to my Court with the goods of their masters to trade, your grace would know that the blacks of your grace are so backward that when we sell slaves to them, they inform us that the slaves were well watched over and captured; they say of them that they are villains they send free slaves to do your service to say to Your Grace that in this my *banza* [capital town] many old free women fled to me as the said people say; of the newer people: If they were here they could make diligent [inquiries concerning the "slave" status of those offered for sale . . .].[14]

Njinga's letters illustrate how African societies were being transformed on account of transatlantic slaving by the mid-seventeenth century. At the time of her death in 1663, more captive Africans departed from the Kôngo-Angola region than the total volume for all other major slaving regions. For African societies in Sudanic West Africa, on the Gold Coast, or in west central Africa, the impact of a burgeoning transatlantic process would be enormous: transatlantic slaving would alter sex ratios and lead to depopulation, create social hierarchies and political fragmentation, introduce new forms of domestic enslavement,

FIGURE 1   The meeting of Queen Njinga Mbande of Ndongo (Angola) and João Correia de Sousa, the Portuguese governor of Luanda, in 1622. (Dutch School, (17th century) / Private Collection / The Bridgeman Art Library.)

---

[14] *MMA*, 12: 289.

and encourage materialist values in societies that valued people above all. But as there are no "slave narratives" for west central Africa, the largest slaving region, we must confront the reality of the sources: the sources we have to provide the enslaved Africans' perspectives are chronologically uneven and geographically rich in some regions and impoverished in others. Our advances in uncovering and extending the range of such sources by historians and archaeologists of Africa, however, belies why neither have not fully utilized life stories by the enslaved, in Africa and its American diaspora, as source material for both the African and diasporic experiences in respective host societies. Using what Pier Larson has called "African narratives of enslavement," we cannot, however, fully probe the social ordering and relations of Beatriz's late fifteenth-century world or the sixteenth- and seventeenth-century world of the *Tarikh al-fattash* and the letters of Mbemba and Njinga. But those narratives allow us to do just that for two important and equally reinforcing mutations of the transatlantic slave system: the full maturity of transatlantic slaving from the eighteenth to the early nineteenth century, and the morphing of this system into increased domestic enslavement and then colonial or debt peonage regimes in Africa and the Americas from the early nineteenth to the mid-twentieth century. As you will see, the volume of narratives published corresponds to the height of transatlantic slaving in the eighteenth century, and contrary to what we might expect, these narratives—at least those crafted in Africa—began to proliferate through the intervention of British naval officials and European missionaries in the nineteenth and first half of the twentieth century. In spite of the missionary, abolitionist, or amanuensis structures that controlled their literary form, African narratives of enslavement, taken together as a genre, provide the closest to a panoramic view of transatlantic slaving, especially its reach beyond "Atlantic Africa" and from those who experienced the almost unending circuit of having, losing, and recreating family and home(land).

During the eighteenth century, the overwhelming majority of published African (and diasporic) narratives of enslavement come from individuals and kinfolks originating between Senegambia and Bight of Biafra along the west African coastline and between 500 to 800 miles into the interior forest and savanna ecologies, in some cases reaching Lake Chad (at the northeastern corridor of present-day Nigeria). To put these distances in perspective, a journey from Timbuktu on the Niger River bend to the slaving ports of Cape Coast or Anomabu in present-day Ghana is appropriately 800 miles; some 900 miles separate Timbuktu from Dakar (Senegal) or Freetown (Sierra Leone), and a sizable number of our narrators hailed from within this radius. For all, the themes of their combined lives radiated with re-occurring capture and renaming, the imposition of one kind of memory over theirs, exile from the cultural self, the use of religion to find or create kin and community (often with cultural strangers), and both the passion and reluctance to return "home" in whatever host societies each found themselves. We will come back to a number of these themes throughout this volume, but the common denominator and most important starting point for these enslaved Africans—and surely for others who remain without a historical voice—was the anchors of family and community in their consciousness and in the retelling of their constrained lives they strove to return to or recreate both.

§

Born around 1710 in present-day northeastern Nigeria, the individual we have come to know as Ukawsaw Gronniosaw (James Albert) began the first page of his account this way: "I was born in the city Bournou [Borno]; my mother was the eldest daughter of the reigning King there, [and] I was the youngest of six children, and particularly loved by my mother, and my grand-father almost [expressed habitual fondness] on me." He was enslaved around age 15 and placed on a Dutch slaver to Barbados by Gold Coast merchants he accompanied from Zaara in Borno, eventually traveling to New York and England where he narrated his account at least 45 years after he left West Africa. His young age and uprooting from his family and kin network must have been pivotal, for Ukawsaw developed an affectionate bond with his first "master" and captain of the Dutch slave vessel, which made his physical departure from African soil possible. But listen to Gronniosaw, albeit decades later and far removed from the immediate feeling of rupture, as he explains his bond with the ship captain:

A few days after a Dutch ship came into the harbour, and they carried me on board, in hopes that the Captain would purchase me. As they went, I heard them agree, that, if they could not sell me then, they would throw me overboard. I was in extreme agonies when I heard this; and as soon as ever I saw the Dutch Captain, I ran to him, and put my arms round him, and said, 'father, save me.' (for I knew that if he did not buy me, I should be treated very ill, or, possibly, murdered) And though he did not understand my language, yet it pleased the Almighty to influence him in my behalf, and he bought me for two yards of check, which is of more value there, than in England. . . . I was now washed, and clothed in the Dutch or English manner. My master grew very fond of me, and I loved him exceedingly. I watched every look, was always ready when he wanted me, and endeavoured to convince him, by every action, that my only pleasure was to serve him well.[15]

For a young man deprived of his "dear mother" and larger kin group, he sought to find a sense of belonging and parenthood, using the same word—fond—for his family and for his first "master," the Dutch ship captain. Whether this bond was genuine, out of pure survival, or short-lived, his natal family and community clearly exercised considerable weight, leaving him with the solace of memory and the secretion of tears: "I often reflected with extreme regret on the kind friends I had left, and the idea of my dear mother frequently drew tears from my eyes." Once across the Atlantic and sold to a second holder, he reminisced of his "father [who] liv'd at Bournou, and I wanted very much to see him, and likewise my dear mother, and sister, and I wish'd he [Mr. Frelinghuysen, a minister] would be so good as to send me home to them; and I added, all I could think of to induce him to convey me back." Ukawsaw would not go home, but what is strange about his account of home was it received about a paragraph's mention, and for the Muslim state of Borno he says nothing of local enslavement or the structure of society or the presence of Islam except a description of an Islamic prayer ("we are oblig'd to be at our place of worship an hour before the sun rise"). Whether he or his family were practicing Muslims it is very difficult to say; if he was raised in a Muslim family, he had deep questions about the belief system he was born into, questions to which his dear mother provided unsatisfactory answers and questions that drove him to willingly leave his homeland with a Gold Coast merchant that eventually led to his Atlantic crossing.

Like Gronniosaw, the enslaved African woman known to us as Belinda says little about her home society, though religion was a central part of Belinda's recollection of home, as she was purportedly snatched (as a child) from a sacred grove while she and her parents prayed. Belinda, who related something of her life at 70 years old and through a petition for personal reparations in the Massachusetts

---

[15] James Albert Ukawsaw Gronniosaw, *A Narrative of the Most Remarkable Particulars in the Life of James Albert Ukawsaw Gronniosaw, an African Prince, as Related by Himself* (Bath, U.K.: W. Gye, 1770), 9–10. See also Vincent Carretta, ed., *Unchained Voices: An Anthology of Black Authors in the English-Speaking World of the Eighteenth Century* (Lexington: The University Press of Kentucky, 1996).

court, was apparently born on the Gold Coast around 1713. Though it is not clear when or on which European vessel she was shipped, she or her amanuensis speaks of "an insulted father" as "she was ravished from the bosom of her country, from the arms of her friends – while the advanced age of her parents, rendering them unfit for servitude, cruelly separated her from them forever!"[16] Dramatic prose aside, her story would have resonated with Ukawsaw and many others, such as Broteer, who left his African homeland through the Gold Coast port of Anomabu. Broteer, who is popularly known as Venture Smith, was born around 1729 and, like Belinda and Gronniosaw, was taken away from family and community as a child and began his account with those who mattered the most. "I was born at Dukandarra [Dubreka?], in Guinea," Broteer related, "about the year 1729. My father's name was Saungm Furro, Prince of the tribe of Dukandarra. My father had three wives. Polygamy was not uncommon in that country, especially among the rich, as every man was allowed to keep as many wives as he could maintain. By his first wife he had three children. The eldest of them was myself, named by my father, Broteer. The other two were named Cundazo and Soozaduka. My father had two children by his second wife, and one by his third."[17] Broteer continues, "The first thing worthy of notice which I remember, was a contention between my father and mother, on account of my father marrying his third wife without the consent of his first and eldest, which was contrary to the custom generally observed among my countrymen. In consequence of this rupture, my mother left her husband and country, and travelled

16 "Petition of Belinda an African, to the Honourable Senate and House of Representatives in General Court Assembled, February 14, 1783," *Revolution Resolves*, 239: 11–14, Massachusetts Archives, 1787; *Acts and Resolves of Massachttsetts*, 1786–1787 (Boston, 1893), 816; "Petition of Belinda, an African, to the Honorable Senate and the Honorable House of Representatives of the Commonwealth of Massachusetts in General Court Assembled," March 5, 1790, in *House Unpassed Legislation*, docket no 3304, Massachusetts Archives; Roy E. Finkenbine, "Belinda's Petition: Reparations for Slavery in Revolutionary Massachusetts," *The William and Mary Quarterly* 64, no. 1 (2007): 95–104.
17 Venture Smith, *A Narrative of the Life and Adventures of Venture, a Native of Africa, but Resident Above Sixty Years in the United States of America. Related by Himself* (New London, Conn.: C. Holt, 1798), 5. For more on Broteer, see James Brewer Stewart, ed., *Venture Smith and the Business of Slavery and Freedom* (Amherst: University of Massachusetts Press, 2010); Chandler B. Saint and George A. Krimsky, *Making Freedom: The Extraordinary Life of Venture Smith* (Middletown, Conn.: Wesleyan University Press, 2009).

with her three children to the eastward." This was the first and its most significant rupture in his life. Broteer's mother would, for unexplained reasons, leave him "at the house of a very rich [unnamed] farmer" where he stayed for two years, "miles from my native place, separated from all my relatives and acquaintances."

During those two years, Broteer, much like Gronniosaw, develops a familial bond with his new "guardian" or "master," the wealthy farmer. Broteer noted, "During my stay with him I was kindly used, and with as much tenderness, for what I saw, as his only son, although I was an entire stranger to him, remote from friends and relatives." Soon, "the difference between my parents had been made up," and upon Broteer's return home, "I was received both my father and mother with great joy and affection, and was once more restored to my paternal dwelling in peace and happiness. I was then about six years old." Rupture, however, came once more, and Broteer and his family would be captured in warfare and his father, Saungm Furro, would be brutally murdered by an invading army. Broteer would spend a number of years in local captivity and then led hundreds of miles to the Gold Coast where he, like Gronniosaw, would be shipped to Barbados, eventually residing in Rhode Island, Connecticut, and New York. What became of Broteer's mother and siblings? We do not know, nor does he tell us. Though it was not unlikely for entire families to have made the Atlantic crossing, surely Broteer would have told us so, especially since much of his physical and emotional labors while enslaved and then emancipated involved securing the freedom of his wife and children—"I had already redeemed from slavery, myself, my wife and three children." Throughout his account, of which one-third focuses on his African experiences, Broteer uses the words "capture" and "prisoner" to refer to his bondage while in West Africa; he only uses the words "slavery," "slave," and "pawn" during his stay in North America, while limiting the meaning of the word "freedom" to a financial transaction and widely employing the word "redeem" when it comes to his and family's departure from chattel enslavement. In the dictation of his narrative and having spent a half a century in North America and with the English language, Broteer's choice of words revealed his own understanding of distinct but familiar experiences of servitude and bondage in the social orders of West Africa and North America.

For Broteer, his movements from kinship to custodianship under a "guardian" to capture and imprisonment under an "enemy" to exportation and enslavement under a "master" held meanings that were at odds, escalating in severity and becoming more fixed the further and further he was removed from kin and from communities with parallel social structures. No one but he could know the exact meaning of "slavery" and "freedom," if there is such a thing, and it is doubtful he or other captive peoples would agree with the false binary notion of "slavery" and "freedom," as if the presence of one means the absence of the other. For even though Broteer also referred to the wealthy farmer as "master," this individual was a different kind of "master" as evidenced by the bonds that ensued and, more importantly, by the fluid nature of Broteer's arrival in the farmer's life by way of his mother and Broteer's departure through the efforts of his father. This open policy of allowing the movement of peoples in and out of social relations—built around processes that transformed strangers, captives, prisoners, and others into quasi-kin—appeared to be quite normal, according to Broteer's account. How normal and how widespread or limited was this policy in various African contexts? Other enslaved Africans from localities and with cultural practices distinct from Broteer's suggest that both limited and expanded forms of kin relationships—where an individual and his or her labor could be used by the custodial family—were the order of the day, but shaped clearly by Islamic and Christian mercantile forces and their localized variations. In this context, pawning and redemption were normal mechanisms for agreements entered into and as a way to satisfy debts; these mechanisms morphed into feeders for the abnormality of transatlantic slaving.

That Broteer used the word "redeem" at least ten times to refer to himself, his family, and "my own countrymen whom I have assisted and redeemed from bondage" indicate that pawning was common for it allowed the individual to remove him- or herself and others from bondage, whereas chattel enslavement placed much of the power of emancipation, except for escape, squarely in the hands of the slaveholder, who could decide for or against so-called self-purchase. In cases involving the pawning of kin on account of debt in African contexts, the pawned individual was usually seized by force and without the consent of the debtor; sometimes the debtor (usually a male) would also be seized, put in chains, and exported from his homeland. It should be noted that the institution of pawning (using valuables or individuals as collateral for credit and the establishment of trust) only contributed a relatively small number of captive Africans to the transatlantic system, since pawns, in the form of gold or humans, guaranteed a loan and theoretically prevented one from being arbitrarily seized and sold on account of a defaulting debtor. In many of the slaving regions in Africa, however, there were few valuables (in the eyes of Europeans) other than people, and European merchants and their agents almost always preferred to trade in humans. The self-identified "Igbo" Ofodobendo Wooma, a contemporary of Broteer from what is presumably Igboland in present-day southeastern Nigeria, argued convincingly that his capture and shipment to the Americas began as pawning transformed by transatlantic slaving: "My father died when I was about 8 years old, and my brother, who was poor and had 5 children of his own, took me to live with him. But not long thereafter, he borrowed 2 goats from a man for 2 years and gave me to him as security. He was supposed to give me back when he received the goats back, but he did not wait for that, he handed me a pipe of tobacco on the road which I trampled underfoot and he took that as cause and sold me to another after a year's time."[18] Wooma would be exchanged several times while still in Africa, but he refers to his holder(s) as both "master" and "companion" and those who shared his captive condition as "servants." Certainly, he and Broteer did not presume that captivity meant enslavement or that enslavement, as found in the Americas, was simply a different name for a similar condition or institution that existed in both their African home and in their host societies.

AFRICAN UNDERSTANDINGS OF "FREE" AND SERVILE STATUS

Categories of "free" and servile status and their meanings and forms across distinct and overlapping African landscapes can be gauged, though generally, from African narratives of enslavement. In some cases, these narratives offer the best set of perspectives—rooted in lived experiences—on the topic. However, the sheer presence of Islamic and Christian mercantile forces and the indigenous people who fell under their spell unfortunately complicates both the panoramic and individuated images we have of African societies as viewed by servile Africans themselves, especially those lives transformed by transatlantic slaving. In this sense, we can surely understand the likes of Ayuba Suleiman Diallo, son of a Fula *marabout* (Muslim religious leader) and

---

[18] Daniel B. Thorp, "Chattel with a Soul: The Autobiography of a Moravian Slave," *Pennsylvania Magazine of History and Biography* 112, no. 3 (1988): 448; see also *Pennsylvania Magazine of History and Biography* 29, no. 1 (1905): 363.

a merchant of high standing who was captured near the Gambia River after failed attempts to exchange two captive Africans to a British slaver and then a successful liquidation of the two to an African merchant.[19] Captured by rivals and sold to the same British ship captain in his first attempted transaction, Diallo was enslaved in Maryland before traveling to England and finally home, where he resumed his slaving activities as an agent for the English Royal African Company (RAC). In 1734, the RAC hoped to use Diallo in its rivalry with the French and their establishments on the Senegal River, and Diallo acquiesced by working in partnership with the RAC. Diallo, in effect, became captive to the very transatlantic slave system, which led to his capture both on the outbound voyages to Maryland and England and on the inbound voyage to his homeland. Equally significant, Diallo and his story embodied the jostling forces of Islam and Christianity in the life of the enslaved, and in the very organization of local African forms of enslavement (where Islam was present), and in transatlantic slaving and the locus of its Atlantic abolition (where Christianity was present).

In the end, Diallo remained a "moderate" Muslim who accepted the principles of—but did not convert to—Christianity while learning English and living among the elite in England. Diallo also accepted the commercial gospel of his former English enslavers by working for the RAC, Britian's principal slaving company. Certainly at the level of theological principles, Islam and Christianity had much in common, and wherever the Islamic idea of the "infidel/unbeliever" and the Christian idea of the "heathen/heretic" converged in African contexts, the target of such allied forces were usually non-Muslim and non-Christian Africans.[20]

---

[19] Boubacar Barry, *Senegambia and the Atlantic Slave Trade* (New York: Cambridge University Press, 1998), 124. Though we are not certain if Diallo was a *marabout* like this father, it is not improbable since such individuals were significant in number and observers in Senegambia were fairly accurate in their descriptions of the "marabout." See, for instance, excerpts of the unpublished manuscript of Louis Moreau de Chambonneau, a late seventeenth-century French administrator, in Carson I. A. Ritchie, "Deux textes sur le Sénégal (1673-77)," *Bulletin de l'IFAN* ser. B. 30, no. 1 (1968): 340-44.

[20] For more on enslaved African Muslims, especially those brought to the Americas, see Allan Austin, *African Muslims in Antebellum America: Transatlantic Stories and Spiritual Struggles* (New York: Routledge, 1997) and the companion *African Muslims in Antebellum America: A Sourcebook* (New York: Garland, 1984); Sylviane Diouf, *Servants of Allah: African Muslims Enslaved in the Americas* (New York: New York University Press, 1998); Michael Gomez, *Black Crescent: The Experience and Legacy of African Muslims in the Americas* (New York: Cambridge University Press, 2005).

Most likely the latter were represented by the two captive Africans whom Diallo exchanged on the Gambia River and certainly many more of these individuals once Diallo brokered an alliance with the RAC. How do we explain this state of affairs? According to European accounts and Diallo's letters, one of which he wrote to his father "hoping he might yet find means to redeem him" while enslaved, the laws of Diallo's hometown stipulated "no Person who flies thither [i.e., Futa Toro along the Senegal River] for protection shall be made a slave. This privilege is in force there to this day, and is extended to all in general, that can read and know God [i.e., Muslims]."[21] And in Diallo's understanding of his society, other Islamic states, and largely non-Muslim polities, only Islam could theoretically provide a modicum of protection against enslavement, though he, a Muslim, was probably captured and sold into Atlantic slavery by fellow yet rival Muslims (we are told his captors were "Mandingoes" [Manding], who are largely Muslim). We are also told Diallo found his two wives and four children when he returned home, but what kind of Muslim did they find in him and what kind of homeland did he now perceive through the optic of the formerly enslaved? Though worthy, we have no way of answering the first, but to the second part of the question, Diallo revealed this: "when he [Diallo] was informed that the King of Futa had killed a great many of the Mandingoes upon his account, he said, with a good deal of concern, if he had been there he would have prevented it; for it was not the Mandingoes, but God, who brought him into a strange land [and in bondage]."[22]

A larger theme of Africans' understanding of their societies in the eighteenth century emerges from Diallo's story: neither religion nor rank in society provided sufficient immunity from the predatory nature of transatlantic slaving and its cumulative reach beyond Atlantic Africa and through caravans, jihadists, and general mercenaries and village raiders. In the late eighteenth century, Peter Panah claimed to be the son of the "king of Cape Mersurdo" (in present-day Liberia), who had been educated in Liverpool by "slave-traders," but

---

[21] Thomas Bluett, *Some Memoirs of the Life of Job, the Son of Solomon, the High Priest of Boonda in Africa* (London: Richard Ford, 1734), 14. See also Frances Moore, *Travels into the Inland Parts of Africa, containing a Description of the Several Nations for the Space of Six Hundred Miles Up the River Gambia . . . with a Particular Account of Job Ben Solomon . . .* (London: E. Cave, 1738), 48, 149–51. Frances Moore was a clerk and merchant for the Royal African Company along the Gambia River, where he lived for five years.

[22] Bluett, *Some Memoirs*, 58.

was nonetheless captured by English slavers and shipped to the Caribbean. It turned out that, while in Caribbean, "he met with other slaves from his own country, who immediately recognized him to be their king's son. This fact was moreover proved by the mark he bore on his breast, which is inscribed on all the king's children, to distinguish them from others."[23] Though Peter's claim was accurate, he died in England while waiting to be transported to his homeland. For Sibell, who was also brought to the Caribbean (Barbados to be precise) in the eighteenth century, she, like many others, began her "Africanized English" account with her family, specifically her father, who, like Peter's, was "a great man in [her] country" named "Makerundy." She goes to list what actually made him a "great man" in the society from which she left (which is not indicated in her account): "he have great many slaves, and hire many man – And one of my budders [brothers] was a great man in de fight in my country – my daddy nebber [never] want – he have ground two, tree [three] miles long and hire as many man dat he put de vittles [provisions] in large tubs for dem – When he cut honey, he fill tree, four barrel he have so muchee. When we want good drink in my country we go and cut de tree and de juice will run, and keep some time will make good strong drink [palm wine]."[24] Unfortunately, not even the greatness of Sibell's father offered enough protection to halt or prevent her Atlantic crossing; at times, and as Peter's story shows, it was often the children of "great men" or village, district, and state officials, including religious officials or spiritual leaders, who were the most vulnerable in their societies.

African children, defined here as those humans below the age of 18, were the most vulnerable of all potential captive or enslavable peoples. Their lives revolved around sheer dependency, especially in the years from infancy to adolescent, and the sense of security provided by family and community adults. The further kinship structures eroded from within by conflicts and individual interests and from without by raiding and warfare, the more young people entered the transatlantic circuit. During the eighteenth century, a recorded

---

[23] C. B. Wadstrom, *An Essay on Colonization, Particularly Applied to the Western Coast of Africa, with some Free Thoughts on Cultivation and Commerce; also Brief Descriptions of the Colonies already Formed, or Attempted, in Africa, including those of Sierra Leona and Bulama*, 2 vols. (London: Barton and Harvey, 1795), 2: 269 [no. 784].

[24] "Two narratives of slave women, 1799, written down by John Ford, Barbados," University of Oxford, Bodleian Library, MS. Eng. misc. b.4, fol. 50r.

4.8 million African children embarked for the Americas, two-thirds of which came from western Africa, that is, Senegambia to the Bight of Biafra – the same catchment zone from which the majority of our African narrators originated. In the second half of the eighteenth century, Tallen a "Kissee" (Kissi?), from an area between present-day Sierra Leone and Liberia, Quobna (Kwabena), a "Fantee" from the Gold Coast littoral, and Equiano an "Igbo" from present-day southeastern Nigeria were all captured and shipped from their homelands as children. Through a set of interviews, Tallen (renamed Dimmock Charlton, among other names) related that he was captured at "9 or 10 years of age" in war by the same group claimed by Diallo—the "Mandingos"—and then taken "prisoners of war" with "six other boys of about the same age" to the coast and placed on board a "Spanish slaver."[25] For Quobna, he too was "snatched away from [his] native country, with about eighteen or twenty more boys and girls, as [they] were playing in a field."[26] In about 1770, at age 12, Quobna details the social ordering of his society, the layers of social relationships he developed, and the context in which his capture occurred:

> I was born in the city of Agimaque, on the coast of Fantyn; my father was a companion to the chief in that part of the country of Fantee, and when the old king died I was left in his house with his family; soon after I was sent for by his nephew, Ambro Accasa, who succeeded the old king in the chiefdom of that part of Fantee, known by the name of Agimaque and Assinee. I lived with his children, enjoying peace and tranquility, about . . . two years. I was sent for to visit an uncle, who lived at a considerable distance from Agimaque. The first day after we set out we arrived at Assinee, and the third day at my uncle's habitation, where I lived about three months, and was then thinking of returning to my father and young companion at Agimaque; but by this time I had got well acquainted with some of the children of my uncle's hundreds of relations, and we were some days too venturesome in going into the woods to gather fruit and catch birds, and such amusements as pleased us. . . . [W]e went into the woods, as usual but we had not been above two hours, before our

[25] Mary L. Cox and Susan H. Cox, eds., *Narrative of Dimmock Charlton, a British Subject, Taken from the Brig "Peacock" by the U.S. Sloop "Hornet," Enslaved while a Prisoner of War, and Retained Forty-Five Years in Bondage* (Philadelphia: The Editors, 1859), 4. See also John W. Blassingame, *Slave Testimony: Two Centuries of Letters, Speeches, Interviews, and Autobiographies* (Baton Rouge: Louisiana State University Press, 1977), 325–38.

[26] Ottobah Cugoano, "Narrative of the Enslavement of Ottobah Cugoano, a Native of Africa; Published by Himself in the Year 1787," in Thomas Fisher, *The Negro's Memorial; or, Abolitionist's Catechism; by an Abolitionist* (London: Hatchard and Co., 1825), 120.

troubles began, when several great ruffians came upon us suddenly, and said we had committed a fault against their lord, and we must go and answer for it ourselves before him.

Some of us attempted, in vain, to run away, but pistols and cutlasses were soon introduced, threatening, that if we offered to stir, we should all lie dead on the spot. . . . I began to think that my hopes of returning home again were all over. I soon became very uneasy, not knowing what to do, and refused to eat or drink, for whole days together, till the man of the house told me that he would do all in his power to get me back to my uncle.[27]

Quobna would see neither his uncle nor his father again. Quobna's captors used knowledge of his family and local socio-cultural norms to provide the captives with hope of returning to home and kin, while they traveled closer and closer to the coast for an Atlantic departure.

Some 800 miles east of Quobna's homeland, Equiano, from his "slender observation" as a child, centered his recollections on his natal village, the structure of society, and the rank of his father in it. From this perspective, he offers some insight into the local meaning of "slaves" and "slavery" therein and in comparative perspectives. His words are worth quoting at length:

I was born, in the year 1745, in a charming fruitful vale, named Essaka . . . [F]or every transaction of the government . . . as conducted by the chiefs or elders of the place. . . . My father was one of those elders or chiefs . . . [who] decided disputes and punished crimes; for which purpose they always assembled together. The proceedings were generally short; and in most cases the law of retaliation prevailed. I remember a man was brought before my father, and the other judges, for kidnapping a boy; and, although he was the son of a chief or senator, he was condemned to make recompense by a man or woman slave. Adultery, however, was sometimes punished with slavery or death. . . .

[As an agrarian society in which all engaged in farming,] the principal articles of which, as I have observed, are provisions. . . . We have also markets, at which I have been frequently with my mother. These are sometimes visited by stout mahogany-coloured men from the south west of us: we call them Oye-Eboe, which term signifies red men living at a distance. They generally bring us fire-arms, gunpowder, hats, beads, and dried fish. The last we esteemed a great rarity, as our waters were only brooks and springs. These articles they barter with us for odoriferous woods and earth, and our salt of wood ashes. They always carry slaves through our land; but the strictest account is exacted of their manner of procuring them

---

[27] Cugoano, "Narrative of the Enslavement," 120–23.

before they are suffered to pass. Sometimes indeed we sold slaves to them, but they were only prisoners of war, or such among us as had been convicted of kidnapping, or adultery, and some other crimes, which we esteemed heinous. This practice of kidnapping induces me to think, that, notwithstanding all our strictness, their principal business among us was to trepan our people.

. . . Those prisoners which were not sold or redeemed we kept as slaves: but how different was their condition from that of the slaves in the West Indies! With us they do no more work than other members of the community, even their masters; their food, clothing and lodging were nearly the same as theirs, (except that they were not permitted to eat with those who were free-born); and there was scarce any other difference between them, than a superior degree of importance which the head of a family possesses in our state, and that authority which, as such, he exercises over every part of his household. Some of these slaves have even slaves under them as their own property, and for their own use.

From what I can recollect [wars] . . . appear to have been irruptions of one little state or district on the other, to obtain prisoners or booty. Perhaps they were incited to this by those traders who brought the European goods I mentioned amongst us. Such a mode of obtaining slaves in Africa is common; and I believe more are procured this way, and by kidnapping, than any other.[28]

As crude and ironic support for the above observations, Equiano and his sister were both kidnapped from their natal village of Essaka, their paths crisscrossing along the way to the coast, leading to an eventual separation.[29] A similar fate fell upon John Joseph and his sister, who were snatched as toddlers from "the arms of a dear

---

[28] Olaudah Equiano, *The Interesting Narrative of the Life of Olaudah Equiano, or Gustavus Vassa, the African. Written by Himself,* 2 vols. (London: Author, 1789), 1: 5–7, 18–20, 23–27. See also Olaudah Equiano, *The Interesting Narrative and Other Writings,* ed. Vincent Carretta (New York: Penguin Books, 2003); Karlee Sapoznik, *The Letters and Other Writings of Gustavus Vassa (Olaudah Equiano, the African): Documenting Abolition of the Slave Trade* (Princeton, N.J.: Markus Wiener, 2013); and Robert Allison, *The Interesting Narrative of the Life of Olaudah Equiano* (Boston: St. Martin's Press, 2006).

[29] For those interested in the ongoing debate about Equiano's origins and his life in "Igboland" and elsewhere, see Vincent Carretta, *Equiano the African: Biography of a Self-Made Man* (Athens: University of Georgia Press, 2005); Innocent B. Onyema, *Hail Usaka: Olaudah Equiano's Igbo Village* (Owerri, Nigeria: Davis, 1991); Catherine O. Acholonu, *The Igbo Roots of Olaudah Equiano* (Owerri, Nigeria: AFA Publications, 1989), and the debate between Vincent Carretta and Paul Lovejoy in the December 2006 and April 2007 issues of *Slavery & Abolition* and in the January/February 2006 issue of *Historically Speaking.*

distracted mother" and made "prisoners of war" on board a slave vessel bound for New Orleans. Like Equiano, Joseph's "father being a distinguished [Asante] chief . . . of great strength and agility" was of little help in protecting his children; in fact, and ironically, it was his father's lack of success in war that led "the enemy" to the father's home and to the capture of at least two of his children.[30]

Born very close to Equiano's Igboland and around the time of Quobna's capture, John Jea "of Old Callabar" (Calabar/Akwa Akpa) began his narrative with the uprooting of him and his family, all of whom shared the Atlantic crossing and slaving experience.[31] He wrote, "My father's name was Hambleton Robert Jea, my mother's name Margaret Jea; they were of poor, but industrious parents. At two years and a half old, I and my father, mother, brothers, and sisters, were stolen, and conveyed to North America, and sold for slaves; we were then sent to New York, the man who purchased us was very cruel, and used us in a manner, almost too shocking to relate."[32] Removed from his homeland as a toddler, unfortunately he does not say how this process unfolded or what were the mechanisms of his and his family's capture, for that process or mechanism would have told us something of the society from which they came and of neighboring or regional communities. Be that as it may, what we do gain from Jea's account is the claim to humble social standing—his parents were poor but industrious—and the same was true for Louis Asa-Asa, who hailed from the yet-to-be-identified town of Egie "in the country of Bycla." Asa-Asa, not surprisingly, began his account with his family, and only an indirect connection to "great men" is made: "I had five brothers and sisters. We all lived together with my father and mother; he kept a horse, and was respectable, but not one of the great men. My uncle was one of the great men at Egie: he could make men come and work for him: his name was Otou. He had a great deal of land and cattle. My father sometimes worked on his own land,

---

[30] John Joseph, *The Life and Sufferings of John Joseph, a Native of Ashantee, in Western Africa Who Was Stolen from His Parents at the Age of 3 Years* . . . (Wellington, New Zealand: J. Greedy, 1848), 4.
[31] On Old Calabar, see Stephen D. Behrendt, A. J. H. Latham, and David Northrup, *The Diary of Antera Duke, an Eighteenth-Century African Slave Trader* (New York: Oxford University Press, 2010).
[32] John Jea, *The Life, History, and Unparalleled Sufferings of John Jea, the African Preacher. Compiled and Written by Himself* (Portsea, U.K.: Author, 1811), 3. Jea became a renowned evangelical preacher.

and used to make charcoal. I was too little to work; my eldest brother used to work on the land; and we were all very happy."[33] The mechanism of war eventually led to the "loss [of] a great many friends and relations at Egie; about a dozen. They [i.e., Egie's adversaries] sold all they carried away, to be slaves. I know this because I afterwards saw them as slaves on the other side of the sea. They took away brothers, and sisters, and husbands, and wives." Asa-Asa and his family ran but "kept together," or so he thought: "I ran up into a tree: they followed me and brought me down. They tied my feet. I do not know if they found my father and mother, and brothers and sisters: they had run faster than me, and were half a mile farther when I got up into the tree: I have never seen them since." British naval intervention rescued him from a life of captivity and gave him the "choice of going back to Africa," but Asa-Asa replied, "Me no father, no mother now; me stay with you" (i.e., his English surrogate), yielding to the desire to belong shortly after losing his natal family and his "many friend and relations."[34] Rather than go to the British colony of Sierra Leone to be among former shipmates and other "liberated" Africans rescued by British naval forces, Asa-Asa's choice reflected not only his youth and loss of kin but also his desire for security and perhaps to reconcile memory of the immediate past with a memory to be crafted in an England that clung to ideas of freedom and abolitionism, as if they could only be attained through them.

For those whom Asa-Asa regarded as having landed "on the other side of the sea," they too had to reconcile memory with their condition, and oral history proved to be an innovative recourse for binding kinfolks across several generations—between those born in parts of Africa and their descendants on new soil and in predetermined economic relations. Speaking for many thousands more in U.S. bondage, Peter Wheeler (b. 1789) of New Jersey maintained a connection with his grandfather through his mother's oral histories: "My mother has often told me, that my great grandfather was born in Africa, and one day he and his little sister was by the seaside pickin' up shells, and there come a small boat along shore with white sailors, and ketches 'em both, and they cried to go back and see mother, but they didn't let 'em go, and they look 'em off to a big black ship that was crowded with negroes they'd stole; and there they kept 'em in

---

[33] Mary Prince, *The History of Mary Prince, a West Indian Slave. Related by Herself. With a Supplement by the Editor. To Which Is Added, the Narrative of Asa-Asa, a Captured African* (London: F. Westley and A. H. Davis, 1831), 42.

[34] Ibid., 41–43.

a dark hole, and almost starved and choked for some weeks, they should guess, and finally landed 'em in Baltimore, and there they was sold." Through this family narrative, Peter came to know something not only of his grandfather but also the very nature of transatlantic slaving and its trademark transformation of humans into kinless chattel. "Grandfather used to set and tell these 'ere stories all over to mother," Peter continued, "and set and cry and cry [just] like a child, arter he'd got to be an old man, and tell how he wanted to see mother on board that ship, and how happy he and his sister was, a playing in the sand afore the ship come; and [just] so mother used to set and trot me on her knee, and tell me these 'ere stories as soon as I could understand 'em."[35]

That Peter's grandfather "wanted to see [his] mother on board [the] ship" should not be misunderstood: the child uprooted from childhood and parents was still yearning for mother in the aged body and tears of grandfather, and by transforming this particular pain into an intergenerational story it linked the consciousness of his daughter and grandson with that of his and his early African ancestry. To be sure, as slaveries in Africa came to a close in the late nineteenth and early twentieth centuries, parents related this story of capture and servitude in Africa like Mbotela did to his son, James Juma Mbotela—through verbal transmission in East Africa.[36] Peter's notes on oral history and trans-generational kinship, therefore, were by no means unique, even among those born in nineteenth-century North America and several generations removed—by birth—from an African homeland. James Williams (b. 1805) of Powhatan County, Virginia, recalled, "My father was a slave [and] . . . a native of Africa, and was brought over when a mere child, with his mother."[37] James knew both his father and grandmother intimately and, like Peter, was nourished with stories that provided connective tissue between generations in the temporal and in spirit. But the distance between home and the diaspora on the other side of the sea was also understood, and crossing

---

[35] Peter Wheeler, *Chains and Freedom: Or, The Life and Adventures of Peter Wheeler, a Colored Man Yet Living. A Slave in Chains, a Sailor on the Deep, and a Sinner at the Cross* (New York: E. S. Arnold & Co., 1839), 21.

[36] James Juma Mbotela, *The Freeing of the Slaves in East Africa* (London: Evans Brothers Limited, 1956).

[37] James Williams, *Narrative of James Williams, an American Slave, Who Was for Several Years a Driver on a Cotton Plantation in Alabama* (New York and Boston: American Anti-Slavery Society and Isaac Knapp, 1838), 25.

it made memory of kin and community that much more integral. Without a doubt, efforts to remember family and reconstitute community transformed the Atlantic into a transcendent bridge rather than an oceanic divide. And so it is to the sea, where vessels and villains made their living off the living—through the processes of Atlantic commerce and commodification—that we turn in the next chapter.

FURTHER READINGS

Carretta, Vincent, ed. *Unchained Voices: An Anthology of Black Authors in the English-Speaking World of the Eighteenth Century.* Lexington: The University Press of Kentucky, 1996.

Eltis, David. *The Rise of African Slavery in the Americas.* New York: Cambridge University Press, 2000.

Ferreira, Roquinaldo. *Cross-Cultural Exchange in the Atlantic World: Angola and Brazil during the Era of the Slave Trade.* New York: Cambridge University Press, 2012.

Larson, Pier. "Horrid Journeying: Narratives of Enslavement and the Global African Diaspora." *Journal of World History* 19, no. 4 (2008): 431–64.

Nwokeji, G. Ugo. *The Slave Trade and Culture in the Bight of Biafra: An African Society in the Atlantic World.* New York: Cambridge University Press, 2010.

Thornton, John. "The Origins and Early History of the Kingdom of Kongo, c. 1350–1550." *The International Journal of African Historical Studies* 34, no. 1 (2001): 89–120.

Vessels and Villains: African Understandings of Atlantic Commerce and Commodification

The first object which saluted my eyes when I arrived on the coast was the sea, and a slave-ship, which was then riding at anchor, and waiting for its cargo. These filled me with astonishment, which was soon converted into terror, which I am yet at a loss to describe, nor the then feelings of my mind.

—Equiano

Before leaving the town of Tinmah (Utuma?) near the Niger Delta and eventually boarding the terror-inducing "slave-ship," Equiano remarked everything in the town, "and all their treatment of me, made me forget that I was a slave. The language of these people resembled ours so nearly, that we understood each other perfectly. They had also the very same customs as we. . . . In this resemblance to my former

31

happy state I passed about two months; and I now began to think I was to be adopted into the family, and was beginning to be re-reconciled to my situation, and to forget by degrees my misfortunes."[1] That Equiano, in his condition of captivity in the Bight of Biafra, could invoke a "happy state" as remedy for his "misfortunes" and realistically contemplate adoption into his holder's family speaks to African understandings of family, society, and bondage and that transatlantic slaving converted humans in kinless objects. Equiano was "hurried away" while his "dear master and companion [the holder's son] was still asleep," ending all possible hope of reunion with natal family, village, or reintegration into communities that resembled his own on African soil. Indeed, on African soil, such hopes could have been realized, and for Equiano this could have happened from "the time I left my own nation" where he "always found somebody that understood me" until the time he "came to the sea coast." The languages, and thus cultures, of the various communities he encountered en route to the coast were "easily learned," and "while I was journeying thus through Africa, I acquired two or three different tongues." Multilingualism meant fluency in multiple or related cultures and thus multiple opportunities for re-establishing kin relations and belonging. And for all those who were or came to be in Equiano's position as a captive, they knew that captive peoples co-existed with and within familial structures – for Equiano, "My father, besides many slaves, had a numerous family" – and that, in the period of transatlantic slaving, both children and adults would "look out for any assailant, or kidnapper, that might come upon us; for they sometimes took those opportunities of our parents' absence to attack and carry off as many as they could seize."

The existence of the potential captive and the potential captor make nonsense out of the fictitious but popular phrase that "Africans sold other Africans into slavery." Said another way, this phrase is troubling because the homogenizing term "African" therein contains three false premises: that individuals and groups viewed their own and others as "Africans," that these undifferentiated "Africans" ceded their "brothers and sisters" into "slavery," and that this "slavery" was unproblematically the same as the one in Africa. African behaviors about what we casually call "slavery" confounds our understandings of it, since the villains were and were not Africans at the same time—Equiano too was baffled while writing in England about his and his

---

[1] Olaudah Equiano, *The Interesting Narrative of the Life of Olaudah Equiano, or Gustavus Vassa, the African. Written by Himself* (London: Author, 1789), I: 64–65.

sister's bondage in "Igboland" some 36 years earlier. "I must acknowledge," Equiano admitted, "in honour of those stable destroyers of human rights [i.e., his captors], that I never met with any ill treatment, or saw any offered to their slaves, except tying them, when necessary, to keep them from running away. When these people knew [the two of us] were brother and sister they indulged us together; and the man, to whom I supposed we belonged, lay with us, he in the middle, while she and I held one another by the hands across his breast all night; and thus for a while we forgot our misfortunes in the joy of being together." It might seem absurd that the two men and one woman who seized Equiano and his sister from their home could be honorable villains or, in Equiano's words, honorable "destroyers of human rights." But along Equiano's journey from natal village into the hands of various kinds of villains, these holders seemed more like kin than captors, and Equiano and they understood that localized forms of kin networks co-existed with—and sometimes morphed into— commercial or slaving networks that fed the transatlantic market, hence community watch groups were on the lookout for would-be kidnappers. Thus, after he and his sister were seized and then separated, Equiano "got into the hands of a chieftain, in a very pleasant country. This man had two wives and some children, and they all used me extremely well, and did all they could to comfort me; particularly the first wife, who was something like my mother." Comfort and motherly affection seem to contradict most of our common views about "slavery" in Africa as well as African understandings of this idea. In fact, in Tinmah, Equiano the captive was "washed and perfumed," he "ate and drank before [his female holder] with her son," he was surprised that "the young gentleman should suffer me, who was bound, to eat with him who was free" and that this same "free" son "would not at any time either eat or drink till I had taken first, because I was the eldest, which was agreeable to our custom." No wonder "all their treatment" made Equiano "forget that [he] was a slave."

Equiano knew well enough that his culture of commerce had changed drastically to a commerce in cultural beings when he boarded that river-bound canoe, eventually leading to a British slave ship, itself transformed from a commercial or luxury vessel into a machine of terror – the same terror Equiano aptly recalled before and after boarding. Listen to Equiano:

I was carried on board. I was immediately handled and tossed up to see if I were sound by some of the crew; and I was now persuaded that I had gotten into a world of bad spirits, and that they were going to kill me. Their complexions too differing so much from ours, their long hair, and the language they spoke, (which was very different from any I had ever heard [on African soil]) united to confirm me in this belief.

Indeed such were the horrors of my views and fears at the moment, that, if ten thousand worlds had been my own, I would have freely parted with them all to have exchanged my condition with that of the meanest slave in my own country. When I looked round the ship too and saw a large furnace or copper boiling, and a multitude of black people of every description chained together, every one of their countenances expressing dejection and sorrow, I no longer doubted of my fate; and, quite overpowered with horror and anguish, I fell motionless on the deck and fainted. When I recovered a little I found some black people about me, who I believed were some of those who brought me on board, and had been receiving their pay; they talked to me in order to cheer me, but all in vain. I asked them if we were not to be eaten by those white men with horrible looks, red faces, and loose hair. They told me I was not; and one of the crew brought me a small portion of spirituous liquor in a wine glass; but, being afraid of him, I would not take it out of his hand. One of the blacks therefore took it from him and gave it to me, and I took a little down my palate, which, instead of reviving me, as they thought it would, threw me into the greatest consternation at the strange feeling it produced, having never tasted any such liquor before. Soon after this the blacks who brought me on board went off, and left me abandoned to despair. I now saw myself deprived of all chance of returning to my native country, or even the least glimpse of hope of gaining the shore, which I now considered as friendly; and I even wished for my former slavery in preference to my present situation, which was filled with horrors of every kind. . . .[2]

Having only encountered the beginnings of his transatlantic voyage, Equiano's wish for his "former slavery in preference to [his] present situation, which was filled with horrors of every kind," was not simply exaggeration as a rhetorical device. He knew the interior corridors of African captivity since he lived it, but he also knew—and appropriately interpreted—transatlantic slaving as another cultural and commercial "world of bad spirits," filled with the currency of "spirituous liquor" and commodified "black people" terrifyingly "deprived of all chance of returning" home.

For Equiano and his fellow captives the terror and an embarkation into the world of kinlessness had only begun, for transatlantic slaving was a surgical procedure premised on severance with the rustiest of

---

[2] Equiano, *Interesting Narrative*, I: 70–73.

chains and the scalpel of violence and fear. "At last," Equiano sighed, "when the ship we were in had got in all her cargo, they made ready with many fearful noises, and we were all put under deck. . . . The stench of the hold while we were on the coast was so intolerably loathsome, that it was dangerous to remain there for any time, and some of us had been permitted to stay on the deck for the fresh air; but now that the whole ship's cargo were confined together, it became absolutely pestilential." This kind of thick description of the Atlantic crossing from the perspective of the enslaved is indeed rare, and thus Equiano's words are worth quoting at length:

> The closeness of the place, and the heat of the climate, added to the number in the ship, which was so crowded that each had scarcely room to turn himself, almost suffocated us . . . and brought on a sickness among the slaves, of which many died. . . . This wretched situation was again aggravated by the galling of the chains, now become insupportable; and the filth of the necessary tubs, into which the children often fell, and were almost suffocated. The shrieks of the women, and the groans of the dying, rendered the whole a scene of horror almost inconceivable. . . .
>
> Often did I think many of the inhabitants of the deep much more happy than myself. I envied them the freedom they enjoyed, and as often wished I could change my condition for theirs. Every circumstance I met with served only to render my state more painful, and heighten my apprehensions, and my opinion of the cruelty of the whites. . . . One day, when we had a smooth sea and moderate wind, two of my wearied countrymen who were chained together (I was near them at the time), preferring death to such a life of misery, somehow made through the nettings and jumped into the sea: immediately another quite dejected fellow, who, on account of his illness, was suffered to be out of irons, also followed their example; and I believe many more would very soon have done the same if they had not been prevented by the ship's crew, who were instantly alarmed. Those of us that were the most active were in a moment put down under the deck, and there was such a noise and confusion amongst the people of the ship as I never heard before, to stop her, and get the boat out to go after the slaves. However two of the wretches were drowned, but they got the other, and afterwards flogged him unmercifully for thus attempting to prefer death to slavery. In this manner we continued to undergo more hardships than I can now relate, hardships which are inseparable from this accursed trade. Many a time we were near suffocation from the want of fresh air, which we were often without for whole days together. This, and the stench of the necessary tubs, carried off many. . . .[3]

---

[3] Equiano, *Interesting Narrative*, I: 70–73.

By now, Equiano was "more persuaded than ever that [he] was in another world." It is that world in Equiano's narrative and in other Africans' understanding of Atlantic commerce and commodification that is the central concern of this chapter.

This chapter picks up where the previous ended by examining various African systems of commerce and their local, regional, and even transnational character, and how these experiences prepared Africans for or departed from the dynamics of Atlantic commerce and commodification. It is important to grapple with African understandings of commodification and not simply their exchange of human and nonhuman commodities, for commodification of African humanity was deeply crucial to transatlantic slaving and represented new forms of dehumanization and homogenization—where a multitude of peoples were smashed into new identities as "Negroes" or "Africans" or "Igbos"—at a time when most African societies valued people above property and goods and where most European merchants involved in transatlantic slaving were accepting "payment" almost exclusively in humans. In the transformation of Africans into captives and then commodities and laboring chattel, the villains were manifold, and so too the vessels or the modes of transport within and from homelands to a diaspora and from individuals who could write their own destinies to ones with subjugated fates. This state of affairs also meant that a number of African states became more stratified and local communities commodified, so much so that a number of decentralized peoples were transformed into slave-trading communities. African understandings of these transformations are central to wider concerns of Atlantic human trafficking and commodification within the entangled histories of Europe, Africa, and the Americas.

AFRICAN SYSTEMS OF COMMERCE

Africa's long-standing trans-Saharan, Mediterranean, Red Sea, and Indian Ocean trade connected its peoples from primarily northern and eastern Africa with those from the Mediterranean world and western and southern Asia.[4] Transatlantic slaving was built upon these

---

[4] On Indian Ocean and trans-Saharan commerce in Africa and world history, see, respectively, Edward A. Alpers, *East Africa and the Indian Ocean* (Princeton, N.J.: Markus Wiener Publishers, 2009) and Ralph A. Austin, *Trans-Saharan Africa in World History* (New York: Oxford University Press, 2010).

previous commercial systems. Because of the endurance of Africa's historic relations with Eurasia through these trade networks, transatlantic slaving would surpass rather than replace them, even as the global economy gradually shifted from the Indian Ocean world in the east to the Atlantic Ocean world in the Western Hemisphere. The world of transatlantic slaving began in the late fifteenth century and reached its height in the eighteenth century, but this global system of enslavement was not unique in its oceanic formation or in its stubborn reliance on captive labor and what they produced. By the early thirteenth century, Genoese and Venetian merchants had already established slaving ports using captive "Slavs" and other peoples to produce sugar for export within a commercial system that stretched from the Atlantic, through the Mediterranean, and to the Black Sea. This "Italian" model of plantation slavery was soon used by Portugal and Spain, expending it to islands off the northwest and west central African coast (e.g., Madeira Islands, São Tomé, and Príncipe) in the late fifteenth and sixteenth centuries. The Ottoman capture of Constantinople (present-day Istanbul) in the late fifteenth century diverted the flow of eastern Mediterranean and Black Sea captives, including Christian Europeans sold by their countrymen, to the lands of Islam. This led to an "Africanization" of the commerce in enslaved peoples, as Portugal and Spain came to dominate the transatlantic slave system until the mid-seventeenth century and as Britain and Portugal would continue that dominance until the first decade of the nineteenth century. The Portuguese and Spaniards would control the trafficking in captive Africans after international slaving was decreed illegal until the end of the nineteenth century—the charter generation of European slavers ended where and how they started.

The vast majority of enslaved Africans were clustered in and exported through major ports that dotted the 4,000-mile coastline from Senegambia to the Kôngo-Angola region in west central Africa and in southeast Africa during the nineteenth century. We should not, however, conflate regions of embarkation with regions or ports of origin; many captive Africans were drawn from political and, at times, religious areas wider and more inland than the major coastal ports, some traveling hundreds of miles to the coast on foot. We could certainly imagine thousands of captive families and friends seized between the vast and varied landscape between the Niger River in West Africa and the Kôngo River in west central Africa and being led through forests, woodlands, rocky pathways, and river water to the Atlantic. A number of these paths on which captives traveled were new, but many were created long before this trafficking by those engaged in local, regional, and, in some cases, transnational commercial networks. Most African societies forged mixed economics where pastoralism, agriculture, fishing, and some mining were woven into the fabric of communities that varied from independent and interdependent villages to states and kingdoms with dependent communities within and those on their internal frontiers. In all, a diversity of food crops (supplemented by animal and fish protein), metals, cloths, leather and wood works, and other commodities were central and often exchanged for locally produced copper, iron, gold (dust), bead, and seashell currencies. Taken together, African commerce was tempered by an unfixed set of relationships—independent, interdependent, and dependent ones— and that commerce hinged on the exchange of various commodities across equally varied ecologies, the least commodity of which was bonded human beings.

This is the general picture we have of African societies inland and along the 4,000-mile coastline until the fifteenth and sixteenth centuries, transformed more dramatically in some places and times than others with the stratifying and slaving effects of Islam in northern and western Africa (especially in the Sahel and savannah regions) and Christian trade and human trafficking through Portuguese nationals in west and west central Africa and in east Africa. External factors such as these and internal factors such as the fight against centralization and stratification provide for a more accurate view of African societies just before and during the transatlantic era. Take, for instance, the Kingdom of Kôngo, which emerged out of the coalescing of smaller, decentralized groups of people and an early economic history involving trade in foodstuffs, cloth, copper, shell, and iron goods and using currencies made from nonconsumable commodities. Indeed, the economies of west central Africa were not wholly dependent on domestic forms of servile labor or slave trading, though the region had extensive commercial markets that could have been used for slave trading and captive laborers did exist. What is important here is that the Kingdom of Kôngo and its capital Mbanza Kôngo (renamed São Salvador in the 1570s) was only one of several socio-political entities, for the region ranged from mobile communities to small villages and polities to full-scale kingdoms of which people became a part or rejected each type of organization based on kinship, association, or residence or on account of spiritual claims and ritual considerations. In fact, the founding of the Kingdom of Kôngo, whose origins dates to the fourteenth century, came down to an alliance that required members of this allied group to socially aggregate and reorganize themselves under a common authority, which had a combined political and spiritual mandate to govern. But this internal movement toward social stratification and political centralization in a vast region did not become widespread until equally large portions of west central Africa fell under the sway of Catholicism and Portuguese slaving and colonization, noticeably through specific inland African rulers and merchants and through the Portuguese colonial states in Luanda and Benguela on the coast.[5]

West central African societies prior to the arrival of the Portuguese generally valued people above property and merchandise. A few decades after Diogo Cão's landfall near the mouth of the Kôngo River in 1483, Portuguese influence and colonization reached as far as Mbanza Kôngo and later Ndongo (Angola). This influence had two related consequences. First, independent communities and states of various sizes in the region became more stratified as the transatlantic slave system grew and as increasing numbers of predatory groups and local "big men" aligned themselves with Portuguese officials as vassals or intermediaries. Those "big men" of local origin, including so-called "Luso-Africans" of mixed African-Portuguese parentage and *prazeros* warlords (Portuguese settlers with large estates worked by enslaved Africans secured through slave raiding and through their private armies), were dependent on credit extended from the Atlantic to acquire guns and captive Africans. Second, societies using laborers, whether war captives or inherited as subjugated persons, turned into slave-raiding and slave-trading societies. In northwestern Angola, the Imbangala state of Kasanje (ca. 1620–1912), for instance, became a major supplier of European goods to the new series of slave frontiers in the east as well as a key supplier of captured Africans destined for the Atlantic coast of Angola in the west and eventually to the Americas. In both Ndongo and the Kôngo, transatlantic slaving made it possible for people—criminals (by way of real or imagined offenses), kidnapped victims, or captive peoples secured from the interior—to be exchanged for political power in the form of imported European goods and guns, which widened the cycle of violence involved in the importation of captives from the interior and guns from the Atlantic coast. Indeed, if capital was the catalyst for the transatlantic slave system, credit was the driving force that kept it in motion. African participants became

---

[5] On Benguela, see Mariana Candido's *An African Slaving Port and the Atlantic World: Benguela and its Hinterland* (New York: Cambridge University Press, 2013).

addicted to this credit, and this made subjugated peoples with a captive ancestry or "foreign" origins and those under the patronage of another more likely to be exported when their holder had to settle a debt or purchase desired European goods.

For the region that historian Boubacar Barry has called Greater Senegambia—from Mauritania to Guinea-Conakry in the south and Mali to the east—the factors of Islam and trans-Saharan commerce have also shaped the politics and cultural landscape of local societies, but, like west central Africa, in tandem with transatlantic slaving beginning in the second half of the fifteenth century. Trans-Saharan commerce, which linked west to north Africa and the wider Mediterranean world, reinforced state centralization in Wolof and Sereer states in present-day Senegal where a socio-political system of differing hierarchies of rank and caste existed. In those systems, persons with servile status were attached to major family lineages and some to ruling families as "royal slaves," though there is no evidence of this until the seventeenth century. But commercially prosperous towns linked to trans-Saharan commerce, such as Jenne-Jeno and its surrounding areas, resisted centralization until the arrival of Islam, which brought to the region a stratified political-religious order where Islam certified local and trans-Saharan slavery and where non-Islamic people, like the non-Christians in a Catholicized Kôngo-Angola region, became prey for predatory, jihadist states. Indeed, those states formed through *jihad* ("holy war") reformist movements led by African Muslims ended up slaving and exploiting captives in more systematic ways.[6] Though indirectly connected to trans-Saharan trade and less affected by Islam, the Akan polities a thousand miles southeast of Senegambia were a mixture of independent communities with centralizing tendencies well before the sixteenth century, but with robust local food- and gold-producing economies that tapped the resources of the dense, tropical forest. Neighboring the Gold Coast were important forest-based and coastal societies engaged in regional commerce by land and along the Atlantic littoral.

On the eastern end of West Africa, Igbo communities such as the settlement of Igbo-Ukwu maintained a noncentralized organization of large and dense populations and local economies for centuries well into the transatlantic era. Like parts of the Kôngo-Angola region,

---

[6] Martin A. Klein, "Slavery and the Early State in Africa," *Social Evolution & History* 8, no. 1 (2009): 182.

however, trade networks such as those under Aro merchants, for whom the vast majority of captives were Igbo and Ibibio, became the primary slave raiding and exporting vehicles in the Bight of Biafra that fed the transatlantic slave system from the mid-seventeenth century onward.

As was true in west central Africa, the Gold Coast, and other major slaving regions bordering the Atlantic, so too did Aro "big men" become patrons for noncaptive and non-Aro individuals who sought their protection and integration into Aro society – patronage was the latter's only way to "become" Aro and thus reduce the risk of exportation. Equiano referred to these "foreigner" Aro merchants as "Oye-Eboe" (*onye Ìgbò*) and was most likely enslaved and exported by them through the port of Bonny. In all of the above parts of Africa, forms of captivity were not central to social ordering and social evolution; a "slave mode of production" and clear distinctions between the enslaved and the enslaver did not really exist, though dependencies related to kinship persisted well into the later centuries.

From Senegambia to west central Africa, and certainly southeast Africa in the nineteenth century, transatlantic slaving grew out of Africa's earlier connections with Eurasia in terms of a commercial network and from captive plantation labor regimes in and around the Mediterranean, shifting from the east to the Atlantic by the fifteenth century. By then, innovations in maritime commerce, in ship construction and navigation, in grasping the temperament of ocean currents and trade winds, in expelling one's foreign (read: Muslim) overlords, and in consolidating racial and religious ideas into the ubiquitous trademarks of "negroes" or "black barbarians"—who were now the objects of conquest, commerce, and conversion—all came together to benefit the Iberian siblings of Spain and Portugal. In Iberia of the mid-fifteenth century, the terms *negro/negra* (and later, *prêto*, describing "black" skin complexion) became synonymous with "slave" (*escravos*) in the same way the term for "slave" (*'abd*, pl. *'abid*) in a number of Arabic dialects became a synonym for Africans. In fact, it was the agreement between Iberian and Islamic racial-religious thinking about deviants from their respective cultural and religious norms, encoded in language and in law, that enshrined Africans as "blacks" *and* "slaves." In effect, "Europeans" with the influence to do so made themselves and others like them into "free-white-Christians" and Africans (or "Negroes") into "enslaved-black-pagans" in Europe, Africa, and the Americas. These transformations from within and applied to those "others" from without would shape the very course and context of Atlantic slaving and commodification.

COMMODIFICATION AND TRANSATLANTIC TRANSFORMATIONS

If African conceptions of personhood included ideas of "wealth in people" and in valuing people over property—though a person may "belong" to or "serve" under another—how did Africans who became captives and then commodities view these transformations? In their journeys to the coast, were they aware of when and how the shift from agent to object occurred? If they were attuned to the structural contradictions of international slaving and its localized forms in the Americas and Africa, what insights did they generate and what action did they take, on whatever scale, against them? Invariably, the African and diasporic lives of those who left a record of their captivity offer unique perspectives, but these perspectives crisscrossed the Atlantic like the travels of Equiano and Mohammed Ali ben Said and, more importantly, provide us with the closest thing to a panoramic window in which to envision their lives.

For coerced African travelers of the Atlantic between the seventeenth and nineteenth centuries, the centrifugal force of transatlantic slaving moved them decisively away from kin and community and filled the ensuing chasm with a life shaped by commoditization. Eighteenth-century captives like Boyrereau Brinch knew commodification began with his capture and removal at age 16 and thought he "courted death, [the thought of] home would force upon me with all its delights and hope." After embarking from an unnamed port with his "comrades" (those "poor African wretches" below deck) and after meeting a "black woman" who spoke his language upon landing, he remained "afraid of the white man," expecting "the white people would whip me to death, and I wished to die so that I could go back to my father and tell him what kind of beings there is in this country." For Brinch, his journey "into captivity" and his courting of death was orchestrated "by a Christian people, who preach humility, charity, and benevolence," and it was these people who consolidated his commodification by renaming him (in the slavers' idiom) York and then Jeffrey Brace. Commodification by way of naming was a staple of transatlantic slaving; it would conceal or replace how one is remembered, almost severing, with each new name, the person from his genealogy and past. On this score, the renaming of Tallen in the nineteenth century was directly associated with his movement in and out of commodification, as he shifted from Tallen the "cargo" to John Bull "the cabin-boy" on a British anti-slaving vessel to "a prisoner of war" on an "American schooner" that forced the former to surrender and lastly to Dimmock Charlton "the slave" through the deception of a judge in Savannah, Georgia. Though Tallen would assert to his new holder, a French tailor in Savannah, that "he was a free man and could not be sold," he could not escape this holder's snatch nor the conclusion that transatlantic slaving was not simply a series of transactions, but also a series of translations where one identity or set of memories was converted into another.[7]

Later renamed and remembered as Venture Smith, Broteer, like Tallen, was seized and exchanged several times in Africa and upon landing in North America, all the while identifying the villains and the vessels involved and the name that would affirm his commodification and kinlessness. Broteer recalled, "I was taken a second time. All of us were then put into the castle [at Anomabu on the Gold Coast] and kept for market. On a certain time, I and other prisoners were put on board a canoe, under our master, and rowed away to a vessel belonging to Rhode Island, commanded by Captain Collingwood, and the mate, Thomas Mumford. While we were going to the vessel, our master told us to appear to the best possible advantage for sale. I was bought on board by one Robertson Mumford, steward of said vessel, for four gallons of rum and a piece of calico, and called VENTURE, on account of his having purchased me with his own private venture. Thus I came by my name."[8] To be named after the very transaction that signaled his "new" identity as a commodity was only the beginning of what would be an ending circuit, interrupted here and there by yet another transaction. "After all the business was ended on the coast of Africa," Broteer continued, "the ship sailed from thence to Barbadoes. After an ordinary passage, except great mortality by the small pox, which broke out on board, we arrived at the island of Barbadoes; [. . . all those alive were sold] except myself and three more, to the

7 Boyrereau Brinch, *The Blind African Slave, or Memoirs of Boyrereau Brinch, Nick-named Jeffrey Brace...* (St. Albans, Vt.: Harry Whitney, 1810), 72, 74, 123–25; Mary L. Cox and Susan H. Cox, eds., *Narrative of Dimmock Charlton, a British Subject, Taken from the Brig "Peacock" by the U.S. Sloop "Hornet," Enslaved while a Prisoner of War, and Retained Forty-Five Years in Bondage* (Philadelphia: The Editors, 1859), 3–5.

8 Venture Smith, *A Narrative of the Life and Adventures of Venture, a Native of Africa, but Resident Above Sixty Years in the United States of America. Related by Himself* (New London, Conn.: C. Holt, 1798), 12. The "castle" in question was likely what become Fort William. See M. A. Priestley, "A Note on Fort William, Anomabu," *Transactions of the Gold Coast & Togoland Historical Society* 2, no. 1 (1956): 46–48.

planters there." Given all that we know about the Atlantic crossing
for the enslaved, some readers might be surprised by the seemingly
emotionless notion of an "ordinary passage," but by the eighteenth
century, during the height of transatlantic slaving, indeed such cross-
ings had become commonplace. What is surprising still, however, is
the nebulous and very brief reference to and lack of details about the
Atlantic crossing, especially for someone so precise in his recollection
of dates, individuals, places, and key events. Be that as it may, Broteer
arrived in Rhode Island and immediately put to work. He, however,
resists choosing to "wear [his] chain peaceably for two or three days."
In response, his holder threatened him: "I will send you to the West
Indies, or banish you, for I am resolved not to keep you." Broteer
answered, in one of the most powerful and widespread idioms of the
era, "I crossed the waters to come here and I am willing to cross them
to return."[9]

But Broteer's temporal life in enslavement and in freedom from it
would continue to be a series of transactions, coded in the language of
purchase, price, and paid sums of money. By the age of 31, he had been
sold three times in North America, and in his final years he lamented,
almost bitterly, the cost of a "purchased" freedom: "the amount of
money which I had paid my master towards redeeming my time was
seventy-one pounds two shillings. . . . Being thirty-six years old, I left
Colonel Smith once more for all. I had already been sold three different times, made considerable money with seemingly nothing to derive
it from, had been cheated out of a large sum of money, lost much by
misfortunes, and paid an enormous sum for my freedom."[10] Broteer
indeed had amassed some wealth through hiring himself out and, in
turn, acquiring property and over 100 acres of land and his and his
family's freedom from bondage. But it was the very ideas of "self-
purchase" and that he was chattel owing property that undermined
or exposed the illogic of chattel enslavement and the transatlantic
enterprise.[11] We do not know if Broteer was aware of these internal
contradictions, though he certainly exploited them to his and family's
benefit, but certainly other eighteenth-century captives, such as
Quobna Cugoano, had little doubt about the inner workings of this

[9] Ibid., 13, 19.
[10] Ibid., 20.
[11] On the enslaved owning property, including themselves, see Dylan Penningroth, *The
Claims of Kinfolk: African American Property and Community in the Nineteenth-
Century South* (Chapel Hill: University of North Carolina Press, 2003).

enterprise and its transformative powers. Some farmers and fishermen became henchmen and parents became childless, leaving Quobna "thus lost to my dear indulgent parents and relations, and they to me. All my help was cries and tears, and these could not avail, nor suffered long, till one succeeding woe and dread swelled up another. Brought from a state of innocence and freedom, and, in a barbarous and cruel manner, conveyed to a state of horror and slavery, this abandoned situation may be easier conceived than described." Reflecting on Atlantic slaving and local forms of captivity, he made the following comparative observation and astute economic argument about the fundamentals of international slaving and commodification:

Thus seeing my miserable companions and countrymen in this pitiful, distressed, and horrible situation, with all the brutish baseness and barbarity attending it, could not but fill my little mind horror and indignation. But I must own, to the shame of my own countrymen, that I was first kidnapped and betrayed by *some* of my own complexion, who were the first cause of my exile, and slavery; but *if there were no buyers there would be no sellers.* So far as I can remember, *some* of the Africans in my country keep slaves, which they take in war, or for debt; but those which they keep are well fed, and good care taken of them, and treated well; and as to their clothing, they differ according to the custom of the country. But I may safely say, that all the poverty and misery that any of the inhabitants of Africa meet with among themselves, is far inferior to those inhospitable regions of misery which they meet with in the West-Indies, where their hard-hearted overseers have neither regard to the laws of God, nor the life of their fellow-men.[12]

Even those born neither in Africa nor in the Americas, but rather in what Belinda from the Gold Coast called "Scen[e]s which her imagination ne[v]er conceived of – a floating world," such as Ignatius Sancho, had a critique of transatlantic slaving rooted in a religio-economic analysis and in targeting those considered the villains. Born on a slave vessel from "Guinea" en route to Cartagena (Colombia) in 1729 shortly after his mother died and his father committed suicide upon landing, the individual renamed Ignatius was eventually brought to England as a 2-year-old, enslaved orphan. Shipping patterns from Atlantic Africa to Cartagena in the 1720s suggest that Ignatius's

---

[12] Ottobah Cugoano, "Narrative of the Enslavement of Ottobah Cugoano, a Native of Africa; Published by Himself in the Year 1787," in Thomas Fisher, *The Negro's Memorial; or, Abolitionist's Catechism; by an Abolitionist* (London: Author, 1825), 125–26 (emphasis added).

parents hailed from and he was conceived somewhere in the Bight of Benin. As an individual who came to live among the nobility of London, he later wrote:

> I am sorry to observe that the practice of your country (which as a resident I love, and for its freedom, and for the many blessings I enjoy in it shall ever have my warmest wishes, prayers, and blessings); I say it is with reluctance, that I must observe your country's conduct has been uniformly wicked in the East, West-Indies, and even on the coast of Guinea. The grand object of English navigators, indeed of all Christian navigators, is money, money, money. . . . In Africa, the poor wretched natives, blessed with the most fertile and luxuriant soil, are rendered so much the more miserable for what Providence meant as a blessing: the Christians' abominable traffic for slaves, and the horrid cruelty and treachery of the petty Kings, encouraged by their Christian customers, who carry them strong liquors to enflame their national madness, and powder and bad fire-arms to furnish them with the hellish means of killing and kidnapping. . . . I mentioned these only to guard . . . against being too hasty in condemning the knavery of a people who bad as they may be, possibly, were made worse by their Christian visitors.[13]

Though England was the leading slaving nation in the late seventeenth and eighteenth centuries, Ignatius's analysis went far beyond the English slavers and their colonies worked by enslaved African labor. By "all Christian navigators," he would have surely meant Dutch, Swedish, Brandenburger (German), Danish, French, Spanish, and Portuguese merchant-slavers in addition to the British. But all these slavers were bounded by fluid and at times reciprocating commercial relationships, where Portuguese slavers would exchange their captive cargo to Danish buyers and where French merchants in Dutch colonies would procure or provide captives to and from British ship captains. In fact, it was the fluctuating nature of intra-European relations and the policies particular to each that, in part, explains the movement of Ignatius from West Africa to a Spanish colonial city to England and the fact that we possess little to any Equiano-like narratives for the Spanish and Portuguese colonies detailing the interior corridors of transatlantic slaving and commodification of individuals drawn from Africa. The one published exception, however, is the account of Mahommah Gardo Baquaqua, originally from the village of Djougou

---

[13] Ignatius Sancho, *Letters of the Late Ignatius Sancho, An African. In Two Volumes. To Which Are Prefixed, Memoirs of His Life* (London: J. Nichols, 1782), II: 4–5.

in present-day Benin, who was captured and exported to the Brazilian state of Pernambuco in the first half of the nineteenth century.

Rather than depart from the general tone and experiences found in other African narratives of enslavement, Baquaqua's account conforms to and, in some cases, extends the widespread patterns of enslaved African lives found in Portuguese, Spanish, and other neo-European colonies. "[A]s soon as the slaves were all collected together, and the ship ready to sail," Baquaqua tells us, "we lost no time in putting to sea. Whilst at this place, the slaves were all put into a pen, and placed with our backs to the fire, and ordered not to look about us, and to insure obedience, a man was placed in front with a whip in his hand ready to strike the first who should dare to disobey orders; another man then went round with a hot iron, and branded us the same as they would the heads of barrels or any other inanimate goods or merchandize." The threshold of commodification meant that Baquaqua and others "were chained together, and tied with ropes round about our necks, and were thus drawn down to the sea shore. The ship was lying some distance off. I had never seen a ship before, and my idea of it was, that it was some object of worship of the white man. I imagined that we were all to be slaughtered, and were being led there for that purpose. I felt alarmed for my safety, and despondency had almost taken sole possession of me." Once on board and stowed in the "floating world" of the slave vessel, Baquaqua recalled the intimate details of the Atlantic crossing:

We were thrust into the hold of the vessel in a state of nudity, the males being crammed on one side and the females on the other; the hold was so low that we could not stand up, but were obliged to crouch upon the floor or sit down; day and night were the same to us, sleep being denied as from the confined position of our bodies, and we became desperate through suffering and fatigue. The only food we had during the voyage was corn soaked and boiled. I cannot tell how long we were thus confined, but it seemed a very long while. We suffered very much for want of water, but was denied all we needed. A pint a day was all that was allowed, and no more; and a great many slaves died upon the passage. There was one poor fellow became so very desperate for want of water, that he attempted to snatch a knife from the white man who brought in the water, when he was taken up on deck and I never knew what became of him. I supposed he was thrown overboard.

When any one of us became refractory, his flesh was cut with a knife, and pepper or vinegar was rubbed in to make him peaceable (!) I suffered, and so did the rest of us, very much from sea sickness at first, but that did not cause our brutal owners any trouble. Our sufferings were our own, we had no one to share our troubles, none to care for us, or even to speak a word of comfort to us. Some were thrown overboard before breath was out of their bodies; when it was thought any would not live, they were got rid of in that way. Only twice during the voyage were we allowed to go on deck to wash ourselves – once whilst at sea, and again just before going into port. . . . We arrived at Pernambuco, South America, early in the morning. . . .[14]

Soon to be renamed Jose da Costa, Baquaqua "remained in [the city's] slave market but a day or two, before I was again sold to a slave dealer in the city, who again sold me to a man in the country, who was a baker, and resided not a great distance from Pernambuco." Baquaqua would acquire an intangible currency of commerce "whilst on my passage in the slave ship," learning "a little knowledge of the Portuguese language" to facilitate communication between him and his holder, "upon which he [the holder] appeared quite satisfied." The slave-master relationship soon turned sour and "[a]fter a few weeks he shipped me off to Rio Janeiro, where I remained two weeks previous to being again sold. There was a colored man there who wanted to buy me, but for some reason or other he did not complete the purchase. I merely mention this fact to illustrate that slaveholding is generated in power, and anyone having the means of buying his fellow creature with the paltry dross, can become a slave owner, no matter his color, his creed or country, and that the colored man would as soon enslave his fellow man as the white man, had he the power."[15] Indeed, power was part of the slaving equation, but for a "colored man" in a slave society so conscious of a wide range of racially and religiously coded skin complexions to be the measure of who would or could "enslave his fellow man" seems facile and off-target. First, Baquaqua's assessment is based on the inaction of an individual "colored man" rather than the forces of capitalist-slaving which brought him from Africa to the Americas. Second, if we theoretically removed the "white man" from the equation, there is no way enslavement in Brazil or elsewhere in the Americas could exist on the backs or through the pockets of a few anomalous "colored" men, whose powers, if any, were decisively

[14] Mahommah Gardo Baquaqua, *Biography of Mahommah G. Baquaqua, a Native of Zoogoo* . . . (Detroit: Geo. E. Pomeroy & Co., 1854), 41–44. See also Robin Law and Paul E. Lovejoy, *The Biography of Mahommah Gardo Baquaqua: His Passage from Slavery to Freedom in Africa and America* (Princeton, N.J.: Markus Wiener Publishers, 2007).
[15] Ibid., 44, 47–48.

constrained by who they were and the social order under which they operated. Perhaps this is why the "colored" man "did not complete the purchase," while this was a nonissue for the Portuguese baker who purchased Baquaqua and a few others before him. Moreover, Baquaqua's potentially important argument does not make it clear if it is "race," or power, or the "means of buying" that is central to "slaveholding." Race structurally delimited and made deviant the racialized "colored" or enslaved individual; power was relative to what constituted it, how it was employed, and by whom in specific settings; and the means to acquire presupposed neither power nor racialized identification, as the Portuguese baker demonstrated. The issue that the renaming of Baquaqua or the intent of his argument raises is not that difference was new to Africans living captive lives in Africa or the Americas, but that—with access to literacy and idioms rooted in racial thinking—African narrators of the transatlantic era now employed the racially coded languages of their European captors.

The same way in which Baquaqua, Equiano, and many others acquired one or more African or European languages along their coerced travels, those with the greatest and varied amount of travel drew contrasting portraits about the cultural similarities or differences encountered, providing for much self-reflection that would, perhaps, have been unthinkable if they were left alone in their own cultural world. Through language, the enslaved found homes and ways to create new or revive old kin networks, confounding the linear goals of transatlantic slaving—kinlessness, "social death," and a perpetual dependency where slavery became *the* life-support mechanism. Throughout the eighteenth and nineteenth centuries in Africa and the American diaspora, a diverse set of individuals that included the likes of Mohammed Ali ben Said, Selim Aga, Olaudah Equiano, Aneaso, and Ofodobendo Wooma reveal the foregoing in incisive ways. Though Mohammed and Selim hailed from the central Sudan, the western and eastern parts of this porous region fed both the Atlantic and trans-Saharan slaving systems, and thus both individuals offer important comparative perspectives. In Borno at the age of 12, Mohammed first encountered a "white man," who happened to be Heinrich Barth arriving on a large caravan from Fezzan; Barth's presence, of course, "raised a great excitement, particularly among us children, for we had heard fabulous tales concerning them," wrote Mohammed, tales "that the whites were cannibals, and all the slaves that they bought were for no other but culinary purposes." Once captured by the "Kindills" (Tuareg) and made a "slave," the multilingual

Mohammed not only described his initial captors (in English, the weakest of his nine languages) in contrasting terms—"The Kindills spoke a language altogether different from ours"—but he used a racially coded calculation to talk about this next holder: "I was sold to a man half Arab and half African.... Abd-El-Kader, my new master ... beat me very often, because I was becoming emaciated with grief and pining for my home." But did he really desire to go home? Upon Abd-El-Kader hearing who Mohammed's father was, Mohammed's holder began to treat him "with more kindness and consideration afterwards, even promising to send me back to Bornou. I was, however, unwilling to recross the inhospitable Sahara [desert]." The polyglot Mohammed, like many enslaved Africans who crossed the Atlantic, had no words to describe his journey across the sea of sand; instead, as those Atlantic crossers would agree, the Sahara or Atlantic "must be seen and felt to be realized."[16]

Choosing not to return home, Mohammed instead "begged him [Abd-El-Kader] to sell me to the Turks, who I had heard, were very good masters. Accordingly, after I had stayed with him about four months, he finally sold me to a young officer, an Aga in the Pacha's army, named Abdy [Abdy-Aga]." Surprisingly, "shortly before we started for Mecca, I one day found some of my comrades, who were captured with me, exposed for sale in the slave-market of Tripoli.... We shed many tears at meeting, and I wept afresh as they told me of the hardships they had undergone. The Kindills had brought them through their own country, and then they had crossed the desert to Tripoli." Indeed, some of his "comrades" or co-captives with whom he shared an affective bond had died crossing the Sahara, and much like commodified crossers of the Atlantic the "survivors [now in Tripoli] were on exhibition, like so many cattle, to be sold to whoever might offer the price at which they were held." Having decided against returning and having found new kinfolks, the bonds between Mohammed and his "comrades" were so strong he would visit "them daily, carrying them whatever I could get hold of in the shape of food, and frequently depriving myself of my own meals for their comfort." But this story gets better, with an ironic ending. Here, knowledge of

---

[16] Nicholas Said, *The Autobiography of Nicholas Said, A Native of Bournou, Eastern Soudan, Central Africa* (Memphis, Tenn.: Shotwell & Co., 1873), 25–26, 41, 43, 44–45, 52, 55. See also Allan Austin, "Mohammed Ali Ben Said: Travels on Five Continents," *Contributions in Black Studies* 12 (1994): 129–58, which contains an interview and an additional, though shorter autographical account.

the captives' family and, later, of Mohammed's family allows them to be reconstituted into their own kin structure, while all are still captives. Mohammed tells us, "At last the Pacha [title for high ranking civil or military officer], having learned that they were from the best families in Bornou, purchased the whole lot and held them for ransom. Soon after this, I saw them well-dressed, walking the streets of Tripoli. I was anxious for the Pacha to buy me, in order that I might be with my companions, *whom I loved like brothers*; and he, upon learning that I was the son of Barca Gana [a general of 'slave' status in Borno's army], was equally anxious to get possession of me; but Hadji Daoud [his holder] would not part with me at any price." Soon thereafter Mohammed would part with his "companions" en route to Cairo, Egypt, and beyond. Selim Aga, after his capture at "eight years of age," was also reunited with co-captives from the same homeland: "On entering the house of my new master, what was my astonishment on seeing an old acquaintance there, a girl with whom I had an interview a few weeks previous. She, poor creature, had also fallen into the hands of the enemy only a few days before myself. This girl, whose name was Medina, admonished me on this occasion, telling me to do whatever I was desired, assuring me that the white man would not care for taking our lives, that the killing of us would not cost him a thought." Selim thought about escape, but "the fear of being recaptured prevented me."[17]

Selim and Medina were then taken to "the camp of the Turks" to be inspected; the imaginary compares well with the transatlantic experience: "The first thing we were desired to do was to show our tongues, and then our teeth. The rest of our limbs underwent a serious examination also. Having undergone this examination, we were taken back to our lodgings again." After losing all hope of "returning to our native country," both were sold and resold to different "Arab" and "Turkish" holders, but, in another transaction, Selim "had the disagreeable misfortune to see her [Medina] sold to another Turk; thus I was left to suffer alone." Unexpectedly, in ways similar to Mohammed's reunion with and separation from "comrades," Selim reconnects with Medina in Dongola (in northern Sudan on the banks of the Nile River)

---

[17] Said, *Autobiography*, 54–55, 72–77 (emphasis added); Selim Aga, *Incidents Connected with the Life of Selim Aga, a Native of Central Africa* (Aberdeen, Scotland: W. Bennett, 1846), 18–21. See also James McCarthy, "Selim Aga: New Light on his Life and his Explorations in West Africa," *The Journal of the Hakluyt Society* (2007), http://www.hakluyt.com/journal_articles/2007/Selim_Aga.pdf (accessed 27 October 2012).

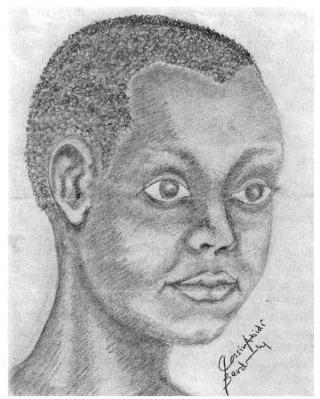

FIGURE 2   A portrait of Selim Aga at age 10 by Yassir Abidi Berdewil. The illustration was drawn in 2007 based on Richard Burton's description. (Used with permission of the artist.)

under new holders and with a new friend: "Salama and I became great friends, and often went together to play by the water side. After the shop was shut one evening, we traced our steps, as usual, to the river's side, but what was my singular astonishment on perceiving a female at a distance whom I thought I knew. On going up to her, whom should I see but my old friend, Medina. Salama stood quite astonished when *he heard her call me her brother*. . . . Medina took us to her master's house, and introduced us to her fellows, but our time being limited, we [promised] . . . to return and see them again. This was a thing which we never accomplished while together, for Salama was sold soon after." Under captivity in Africa or the American diaspora, kin relations and the bonds that hold them together were always moving targets; but captive or not, Selim was determined to maintain those bonds with Medina, and so he would "pay another visit to Medina, who always gave me a kind reception, and had a little more time to relate our respective histories. I found that I was with my seventh master, whilst she was only with her fifth. Our time being so uncertain, we always bid each other good bye forever, and it proved so on this occasion. Two or three days after, my master brought a man to the shop, who carefully scrutinized me after the manner of the slave traders, and then I was desired to follow him as my future owner." With uncertainty the constant variable, Selim was not even allowed to say "farewell [to his] fellow slaves who were at the house, [but] was obliged to abandon everything and follow him."[18]

Selim's "everything" revolved around his relationship with Medina and with co-captives found along the way. Ironically, his departure came by way of a slave ship traversing the Nile River: "The slave-ship landed in its season at Goortie [town in the Dongola region], and took us on board. We arrived at the first cataracts of the Nile, and it being impracticable for the ship to proceed farther, we had to change our quarters. The masters busied themselves looking out for another ship to contain their menagerie of human beings. For this purpose we had to travel by land, and finally to sleep on land, before embarking again." Eventually he would be sold to his ninth holder, Robert Thurburn, the British commercial consul in Egypt, who would return to England with Selim. Time and circumstances made it impossible that Selim would have met Mohammed and even less likely Equiano in England, but Equiano and both captive travelers of the sea of sand had much in common and would have had much to talk about at a hypothetical meeting. They, like Equiano and other "Igbo" individuals, experienced the inspections prior to departure and upon arrival and the meeting of kin or acquaintances: "They put us in separate parcels," wrote Equiano, "and examined us attentively. They also made us jump, and pointed to the land, signifying we were to go there. We thought by this we should be eaten by these ugly men. . . . [A]t last the white people got some old slaves from the land to pacify us. They told us we were not to be eaten, but to work, and were soon to go on land, where we should see many of our country people." And soon "there came to us Africans of all languages," allowing multilingual people to seek reunion or build new relations through clustered and, at times, mutually intelligible idioms.

---

[18] Ibid., 20–21, 28–29 (emphasis added).

Equiano, Selim, and Mohammed knew all too well their commod-ification and homogenization into "blacks," "negroes," and "Africans": "We were conducted immediately to the merchant's yard, where we were all pent up together like so many sheep in a fold, without regard to sex or age." But in the herding of these captives, there was an inter-nal dialogue taking place, a dialogue of intra-African understanding and of forging communities. "While I was in this astonishment [of seeing people on horseback]," noted Equiano, "one of my fellow pris-oners spoke to a countryman of his about the horses, who said they were the same kind they had in their country. I understood them, though they were from a distant part of Africa, and I thought it odd I had not seen any horses there; but afterwards, when I came to con-verse with different Africans, I found they had many horses amongst them, and much larger than those I then saw."[19] Far from fictive, these relations were very real and terribly important as a combined fight against commodification and its imposition of a "slave" memory and identity on the captive. In the end, Equiano became Gustavus Vassa and a Christian, Selim kept his indigenous name but he and Mohammed (renamed Nicholas Said) became Christians, fellow self-described "Igbo" Ofodobendo Wooma (renamed York and then Andrew) became a Christian, another "Igbo," Aneaso (renamed Toby and then Archibald John Monteith), became one of the "attractive articles of merchandise" he saw on the coast and later a Christian in Jamaica, and, lastly, the Muslim Omar ibn Said of the Carolinas, who claimed "wicked men took me by violence and sold me to the Christians," became a Christian and remembered as Uncle Moreau, among other renditions.[20] The transformation of these individuals,

[19] Equiano, *Autobiography*, I: 84–86.
[20] Equiano, *Autobiography*; Mary Prince, *The History of Mary Prince, a West Indian Slave. Related by Herself. With a Supplement by the Editor. To Which Is Added, the Narrative of Asa-Asa, a Captured African* (London: F. Westley and A. H. Davis, 1831), 43; "Autobiographical Sketch of Archibald Monteith," in Thomas Harvey and William Brewin, *Jamaica in 1866: A Narrative of a Tour Through the Island . . .* (London: A.W. Bennett, 1867), 89–90; Said, *Autobiography*, 145; Daniel B. Thorp, "Chattel with a Soul: The Autobiography of a Moravian Slave," *Pennsylvania Maga-zine of History and Biography* 112, no. 3 (1988): 433–51; John Franklin Jameson, ed., "Autobiography of Omar ibn Said, Slave in North Carolina, 1831," *The American Historical Review* 30, no. 4 (1925), 787–95, but see also Ala Alryyes, *A Muslim American Slave: The Life of Omar Ibn Said* (Madison: University of Wisconsin Press, 2011), since this study provides a new English translation facing the Arabic text and essays that correct Jameson's and other misreadings of Said's narrative.

however, was not one-sided: captives, in all their overlapping experiences and shared trajectories, became commodities and chattel, but captors of all stripes became "slaves" to capital and, in turn, became cannibals feasting on human lives—a matter we will take up in Chapter 4. African understandings of these transformations are thus central to wider concerns of Atlantic commerce and commodification, and the incubation of capitalism, within the histories of Europe, Africa, and the Americas. These understandings also have bearing on matters to be explored in the next chapter, which addresses how the "black bodies" of Africans became sites of identity, religious encounters, and vehicles for a spiritual and physical return home.

FURTHER READINGS

Alpers, Edward A. *East Africa and the Indian Ocean.* Princeton, N.J.: Markus Wiener Publishers, 2009.

Austin, Ralph A. *Trans-Saharan Africa in World History.* New York: Oxford University Press, 2010.

Boubacar Barry. *Senegambia and the Atlantic Slave Trade.* New York: Cambridge University Press, 1997.

Eltis, David, and David Richardson. *Atlas of the Transatlantic Slave Trade.* New Haven, Conn.: Yale University Press, 2011.

Inikori, Joseph E. "Ideology versus the Tyranny of Paradigm: Historians and the Impact of the Atlantic Slave Trade on African Societies." *African Economic History* 22 (1994): 37–58.

Rediker, Marcus. *The Slave Ship: A Human History.* New York: Penguin, 2007.

Reinhardt, Catherine A. *Claims to Memory: Beyond Slavery and Emancipation in the French Caribbean.* New York: Berghan, 2006.

Shaw, Rosalind. *Memories of the Slave Trade: Ritual and the Historical Imagination in Sierra Leone.* Chicago: Chicago University Press, 2000.

Smallwood, Stephanie. *Saltwater Slavery: A Middle Passage from Africa to American Diaspora.* Cambridge, Mass.: Harvard University Press, 2007.

Sweet, James H. "The Iberian Roots of American Racist Thought." *The William and Mary Quarterly* 54, no. 1 (1997): 143–66.

Black Bodies at Bay
and Reversing Sail: African
Understandings of Self,
Religion, and Returning Home

Great respect is paid to the aged; they never use the prefix mister or mistress, but
always some endearing term, such as, when speaking to an aged person, they
say Father or Mother, and an equal, they call brother or sister. Children ... bend
their knee to the aged, and the aged in turn bend their knee to them, and request
them at once to rise; and in every respect a deference is paid to age. The best seat
is reserved for them, and in their places of worship, the place next to the priest is
reserved for them.

—Mahommah Gardo Baquaqua

That Mahommah would argue age and not anatomy was a central
criterion for personhood and one's cultural and religious standing in
society should not be surprising. This dispassionate Muslim belonged

to a significant Muslim and commercial family but was reared in an African society where the political leaders and the majority of the populace were non-Islamic and where relative age, status, wealth, and other factors were determinants for personhood and attendant social roles and values. Having traveled to Brazil, New York, Haiti, and Canada—where he related his account less than a decade after he was exported from his homeland—he rhetorically asked, "Should not these facts [in the opening quote] put to shame the manners of the children in this country [Canada] towards the aged? How painful it is to witness the disrespect shown to grown up people by the rising generation of this country, and in many cases the shameful behavior of children towards even their own parents, and that without a single check of censure or rebuke!" This admonishment should also not be surprising. He devoted almost two-thirds of his account to his African experiences, and he had traveled to Portuguese, English, (Haitian) Kreyòl, and English-French speaking territories and therefore had enough empirical evidence to draw such comparisons about the ways age and respect worked between his home and host societies. In recalling his hometown of Djougou, then the largest commercial city in northwest Benin, Mahommah was attentive to the distinct and overlapping roles performed by a range of individuals—father, mother, children, brother, sister, elderly or aged person, priest—but these roles were not "gendered" or reduced to a function of sexuality, hence his shrewd rejection of "mister or mistress" and his preference for more "endearing term[s]" rooted in indigenous self-understandings. In effect, individuals of either (and, in contemporary parlance, any) "gender" could occupy those roles, and where there were specific roles, they appeared to complement another: "The women do the spinning by a very slow process," Mahommah tells us, "having to twist the thread with their fingers; the men do the weaving; they weave the cloth in narrow strips, and then sew it together."[1] Though he tried, we do not know if Mahommah made the return voyage back home; but whether he did or not, his nineteenth-century voice provides one of several perspectives on the cultural self (and on enslaved "black bodies"), on indigenous spiritualities and Islam and Christianity, and of efforts to defy the gravity of the one-way Atlantic crossing by returning to a known homeland.

[handwritten marginalia: Gender roles different]

---

[1] Mahommah Gardo Baquaqua, *Biography of Mahommah G. Baquaqua, a Native of Zoogoo . . .* (Detroit: Geo. E. Pomeroy & Co., 1854), 17–18.

The purpose of this chapter, then, is twofold, which is reflected in its structure. In the first half we draw attention to African understandings of identity during the transatlantic era in contrast to two views: those of European onlookers, who principally interpreted matters of sexuality, gender, and cultural identity through their own religious and cultural lens, and those of "Europeanized" Africans, who sought to refashion themselves, in part or in whole, in terms of "European" conceptions of the aforementioned. These understandings, as articulated through African narratives of enslavement, will help locate the reader in the socio-cultural worlds of the African as to the meaning or usefulness of the above notions and the limitations of interpreting retrospectively current preoccupations with cultural identity and gender. Rather than view notions of gender, sexuality, and cultural identity as ontological givens, they will be treated as theoretical tools to be tested against the lived experiences of enslaved Africans during the transatlantic era. The second half of this chapter explores transatlantic slaving as an uneven set of religious encounters and contests between and among Christian, Islamic, and indigenous African spiritual adherents. African understandings of these important historical processes—and resistance to them—are critical, since those "liberated" Africans who returned to nineteenth-century Africa did so largely as Christianized individuals and proselytes for an "Africa" different from the one they or their ancestors left. Ironically, it was these returnees, sponsored and trained by European missionary organizations, who led the charge for the greater proselyzation and Christianization of Africa.

AFRICAN UNDERSTANDINGS OF CULTURE AND IDENTITY

Matters of identity, sexuality, gender, life, death, and the like are all culturally constructed by humans located in specific ecological, linguistic, and historical contexts. Though we all have human bodies, what it means to be a "woman/man," "wife/husband," "mother/father," or "female/male" is never solely or more importantly a function of biology. Likewise, a woman's (or a man's) sexuality, fertility, and femininity are not distinct ways to talk about the same cross-culture quality or characteristic. If the meanings of these concepts exist in the language of a people, then they would all be culturally coded and would only fully register with speakers and thinkers in that language. The problem, then, is translation—more precisely, translating culture. The ideas of "gender" and sexuality have become synonyms for identity in recent times, but these late nineteenth- and early twentieth-century entrants into the English language would have found little resonance among enslaved Africans, not only because these notions did not exist at the time of their departures in their languages, but also because the phenomena to which they refer have very little evidentiary base in many African societies before the nineteenth century or where there was no European settlement, colony, or trading enclave with significant African–European interactions. For instance, studies on male homosexuality in the transatlantic era found "precious little evidence describing the role of transvested homosexuals in sixteenth- and seventeenth-century Africa," and where there is suggestive and stronger evidence, it is found, respectively, in west central Africa where Portuguese settler colonies exercised significant influence and in twentieth-century data coming largely out of south(ern) Africa, another region of large-scale European settler colonies.[2] There is thus enough reason to temper the urge by some to project their present-day concerns with and understandings of sexuality or gender into a past where these ideas did *not* exist nor could have been the bases for a cultural identity. Indeed, even in the contemporary period, the ideas of gender and sexuality as we know it are not cross-culturally inherent in social relations as a basis of identity, as Mahommah has shown for his time and place. Indeed, these new constructs have been deployed in undiscriminating ways and without much concern for how identity and belonging were based less on biology and sexual organs (or feelings) in much of Africa than on having successfully completed specific rites of human development.[3] These rites of human transition from one phase of maturation

---

[2] James H. Sweet, "Male Homosexuality and Spiritism in the African Diaspora: The Legacies of a Link," *Journal of the History of Sexuality* 7, no. 2 (1996): 191 (quotation); Marc Epprecht, "Sexuality, Africa, History," *The American Historical Review* 114, no. 5 (December 2009): 1268.

[3] On the "gender" debate in African and diaspora studies, see, for instance, Oyeronke Oyewumi, ed., *Gender Epistemologies in Africa: Gendering Traditions, Spaces, Social Institutions, and Identities* (New York: Palgrave Macmillan, 2010); idem, *The Invention of Women: Making an African Sense of Western Gender Discourses* (Minneapolis: University of Minnesota Press, 1997); James Lorand Matory, *Sex and the Empire That Is No More: Gender and the Politics of Metaphor in Oyo Yoruba Religion* (New York: Berghahn Books, 2005), originally published in 1994 by the University of Minnesota Press; Ifi Amadiume, *Male Daughters, Female Husbands: Gender and Sex in an African Society* (New York: Palgrave Macmillan, 1987).

to another often included, but were certainly not limited to, birth and naming, coming of age, and marriage ceremonies. Birth, like all important stations in temporal life, is the quintessential rite of passage to a human existence, but the achievement is never guaranteed and the possibilities for success or premature demise are equally uncertain. But once birth happened, naming ceremonies of some sort usually affirmed the new human addition to the family and community as well as authenticating him or her as a living, cultural member of society. As the child grew toward adulthood, most societies subjected either boys and girls or one of the two to a rite of passage, preparing the young person for the life of an adult. A few years thereafter, he or she was usually expected to marry, as a signpost of adulthood, as preparation for procreation, and as another major rite of human development. Specific ornamentation or mode of dress distinguished married and unmarried women, and for the "Igbo," Equiano noted, a married woman has "tie[d] round her waist a cotton string of the thickness of a goose-quill, which none but married women are permitted to wear." For Mahommah, it is in his recollection of marriage in Borgu—a town of indigenous political elites and a Muslim minority with some influence—where we find that marriage was the "birthing" of another human addition, the extending family, through the joining of two families, represented in this ritual moment by a soon-to-be mother and father who shared this space on mutual terms. Mahommah notes,

> When a young man wishes to marry, he selects a choice fruit called Gan-ran, and sends it by his sister or some female friend to the object of his choice; if the fruit is accepted, he understands that he will be favorably received, and remains at home for about a week before he pays her another visit. After some time spent in visiting and receiving visits, arrangements are made for the marriage ceremony. They do not have a particular day set, and a wedding at the bride's father's, but she is kept ignorant of the time; the arrangements are made by the bridegroom and her parents. At the time appointed, the bridegroom sends a number of young men to the house of her father at night; they remain out of doors very still and send a child in to tell her some one wishes to speak with her. She goes to the door and is immediately surrounded and carried off by the young men, to a place called Nya-wa-qua-foo, where she is kept six days; during this time she remains veiled and has a number of female friends with her, who spend their time in play and amusements. The bridegroom in the meantime confines himself at home and is attended by his young friends, who also spend their time in feasting and merriment until the seventh day.

Whilst they are thus confined, a general invitation is given to the friends of both parties. . . . They all meet at some convenient place named for the purpose. The friends of the bridegroom conduct him there, and the friends of the bride, conduct her also; both bride and groom having their heads covered with white cloths. A mat is prepared for them to be seated; the friends advance and salute the bridegroom, at the same time handing him some money. The money is then placed before the couple, who are thus considered man and wife. Money is likewise scattered for the drum king and his company; also for the children of the populace to pick up. After this, they are conducted to the house of the bridegroom. The ceremonies are thus brought to an end.[4]

Both the "bride" and the "groom" were confined for a number of days, attended by respective friends in preparation for and during the marriage ceremony, and both individuals' "heads [were] covered with white cloths." This all seems egalitarian, but was it really so? Mahommah claims that "polygamy is practiced to a great extent, and sanctioned by law. A man's property is sometimes estimated by the number of wives he has. Occasionally a poor man has a number of wives, and then they have to support him. When a rich woman marries a poor man (as is sometimes the case) he never has more than one wife. Mahommah's mother was a woman of rank and wealth. His father . . . lost the greater part of his property, and at the time of his marriage was comparatively poor; he consequently had but one wife." Though Mahommah was part of a Muslim community, his observations on multiple wives seem accurate for both Muslim and non-Muslim societies, but in either case there were specific cultural and pragmatic constraints that made polygamy far less than a continental phenomenon. For those who participated in the practice, "the men [may] . . . indulge in a plurality," as Equiano observed," but the majority "seldom in more than two." What is important here is that polygamy was not simply the power of "men" over "women" or vise versa; rather, the institution of polygamy was regulated by the "rank and wealth" of women and men. If all that Mahommah has shared was true for the society in which he lived and later recalled, then is it quite difficult to reconcile those perspectives with his (or his editor's) idea that "women in Africa are considered very inferior to the men, and are consequently held in the most degrading subjection," and as substantiation we are told women "never eat at the same table with the men, or rather in their presence, (they having no tables) but in separate apartments."[5] Eating with men

---
[4] Baquaqua, *Biography*, 20–21.
[5] Ibid., 21.

in the *same* place would actually suggest men were the measure of women's places and roles; the fact is, according to Mahommah's own account, both had distinct roles and spaces, and this situation was the norm in a number of other African societies so that Equiano, for instance, was compelled to remark, while a captive in a host African society, "[t]heir women were not so modest as ours, for they ate, and drank, and slept, with their men." Equiano would have been at home in Borgu, but he, and surely others, would not have viewed such culturally tailored and accepted roles at the time of his departure from Igboland as anything more than the specific (and, at times, overlapping) roles, standings, and places occupied by fathers, mothers, children, brothers, sisters, elderly persons, priests, and others. All these social actors remained undifferentiated by "gender"; rather, the organizing principles of age, rites, wealth, rank, and the like were more central to social ordering, but an order where the boundaries created by these criteria were often crossed, as the wealthy woman of high rank would marry the poor man of lower rank.

How Africans ordered their societies tells us about the principles used to craft their identities and how they came to identify themselves and those unlike themselves. Cultural identity derives from the ways in which a people's culture moves through its history and ecology, but also through the decisions made around foundational self-understandings and the more amenable forms of culture, such as material culture, systems of food production, and dress. For enslaved Nuba Selim Aga, nature and culture shaped social roles, and thus, in a society dominated by pastoralism, it was the "junior [rather than the senior] male members of the family employed in taking care of the flock." But where age was not the main organizing principle, then it was the supplementary criterion of dress as a symbol or indication of social standing: "The dress among the higher classes is a long wide gown, reaching to the ankles, and wide open sleeves, so as not to confine the wearer too much, and sandals on their feet. The lower classes, again, have a long wide plaid, which they tie round their body, and over one of their shoulders, leaving the other quite free; while in length it only reaches to the knees. This forms all their variety of dress."[6] If dress was a marker of social identity, then the insignificant variation in Nuba dress as remembered by Selim suggests that the distinction between the "classes" were similar. In the Bight of Biafra, where egalitarian societies existed,

---

[6] Selim Aga, *Incidents Connected with the Life of Selim Aga, a Native of Central Africa* (Aberdeen, Scotland: W. Bennett, 1846), 16–17.

Equiano tells us that the "dress of both sexes is nearly the same. It generally consists of a long piece of calico, or muslin, wrapped loosely round the body, somewhat in the form of a highland plaid. . . . Besides this, our women of distinction wear golden ornaments; which they dispose with some profusion on their arms and legs. When our women are not employed with the men in tillage, their usual occupation is spinning and weaving cotton, which they afterwards dye, and make it into garments. They also manufacture earthen vessels, of which we have many kinds."[7] Both Selim and Equiano offer integral perspectives across one century and across two ecologically different societies that shared similar principles for ordering social identities and the roles that flow from them.

The making of social identities in specific ecologies meant that enslaved Africans recognized similarities and differences between the group to which they belonged and those deemed "strangers," "foreigners," and "enemies." Transatlantic slaving, however, homogenized the varying and overlapping folks along and hundreds of miles behind that 4,000-mile coastline between Senegambia and Angola into "Africans," "Negroes," and "black" people without regard to the ways in which they viewed each other and the criteria for such views. The age of race and racialization had begun, and African narrators of enslavement—who did not write or leave an oral record in *their own* languages—had little option but to use the language of race (and "nation" and "country") to talk about themselves, their societies, those external to them, and their combined experiences. Thus, for the eighteenth century's most well-known "black" writer, Equiano, the word "difference" ran throughout this two-volume account, but in drawing lines between him and "them" he told us something about his identity and that of his "Igbo" peoples. In one instance, Equiano drew sharp distinctions between communities that were culturally similar to and different from his own and the gap between the two poles increased as he traveled to the coast:

> All the nations and people I had hitherto passed through resembled our own in
> their manners, customs, and language: but I came at length to a country, the in-
> habitants of which differed from us in all those particulars. *I was very much struck*
> *with this difference*, especially when I came among a people who did not circum-
> cise, and ate without washing their hands. They cooked also in iron pots, and had

---

[7] Olaudah Equiano, *The Interesting Narrative of the Life of Olaudah Equiano, or Gustavus Vassa, the African* (London: Author, 1789), I: 11–12.

European cutlasses and cross, bows, which were unknown to us, and fought with
their fists amongst themselves. . . . But, above all, I was amazed to see no sacrifices
or offerings among them. In some of those places the people ornamented themselves with scars, and likewise filed their teeth very sharp. They wanted sometimes
to ornament me in the same manner, but I would not suffer them; hoping that
I might sometime be among a people who did not thus disfigure themselves, as
I thought they did. . . . The chief employment in all these countries was agriculture,
and both the males and females, as with us, were brought up to it, and trained in
the arts of war.[8]

Though Equiano knew that the primary mode of subsistence and
surplus wealth was agrarian life among "the males and females" of
analogous and diverse societies, including those he came upon, it is
his comparative perspective that is of greater empirical value. In his
analysis, Equiano drew attention to the ways in which a number of
Africans understood cultural difference and thus group identity –
that is, we are who we are because of what we have *and* what we have
not become. By this logic, Equiano could easily and appropriately
discern those cultures that "resembled our own" and those that "differed from us," while simultaneously expecting to see what he knew
("I was amazed to see no [ritual] sacrifices or offerings among them")
or refusing to undergo the manner (rather than the practice) of scarification and adornment ("I would not suffer them"). However, these
self-understandings were neither the "ethnicity" nor the language of
"race" that Europeans in and around the Atlantic preferred.

The matrices for these understandings of self and others—which
should not be confused with the anthropological understanding of
"the other"—were found in language and in spirituality, which will be
discussed shortly. Language at the level of greetings was central to
human relations in many African societies, and thus how and who one
greets offered not only an affirmation of their existence but also the
cultural identity of the greeter and the greeted. Most cultural groups
and familial clans possessed "praise names" and specific procedural
salutations by which members of the group greeted each other, and it
was in this context that the formerly enslaved Samuel Ajayi Crowther
made some relevant observations after British naval intervention

---

[8] Ibid., 66–70 (emphasis added). Fellow, self-described "Igbo," Ofodobendo Wooma,
was circumcised at 8 years old "according to the custom of my nation" and was forbidden to eat pork, among other cultural regulations. See Daniel B. Thorp, "Chattel
with a Soul: The Autobiography of a Moravian Slave," *Pennsylvania Magazine of
History and Biography* 112, no. 3 (1988): 447.

thwarted his Atlantic crossing and brought him and other "liberated" Africans to Freetown, Sierra Leone, in the late 1820s. According to Crowther, who produced perhaps the first Yorùbá dictionary and grammar, the "Eyo or Yorùbá is called Aku" in salutation (and become known as "Aku" in Sierra Leone), but the Yorùbá "is called Ayaji by the Nupe," "Yariba [or Yaraba] by the Hanssa [Hausa]," "Anagonu or Inago by the Popo," and "Ayonu by the Dahomey." In turn, the Yorùbá called the Nupe "Tapa or Takpa," "Popo is called Egun," and "Dahomey is called Dada."⁹ As Crowther's taxonomy shows, African societies were self-conscious of their own authored group identity (endonym) and how they were identified by others (exonyms) in Africa, but it also demonstrates how, for instance, the Hausa ethnonym "Yariba" (Yaraba) became the exonym "Yorùbá," which has defined a language and a people for the past few centuries. Finally, the perspectives of Equiano and Crowther indicate how so-called African "ethnicities" co-existed with—but were later superseded by—the racial homogenization of Africans, enslaved or not, and how race, in sometimes caricaturized forms, would become the language of identification and identity. Ignatius Sancho, who was born on a slave ship in 1729 and thus had no "African" experience per se, explained himself to the world in these terms: "I am, as much as a *poor* African can be," an "African" who "can't help the place of his nativity," and "a *coal-black*, jolly African."¹⁰ Likewise, the polyglot Mohammed Ali ben Said, an enslaved Kanuri of the nineteenth-century Atlantic world, chose to write his autobiography in the language of race, for instance, "The Tibbous are *black*, with features more regular than those of the Kanouries [Kanuri]. Their customs are similar to our own, but they speak a dialect unintelligible to both us and the Kindills [Tuaregs]."¹¹ In effect, the race signifier "blackness" became a fixed synonym for "African" and "slave." Both "slave" and "African," in Arabic dialects and numerous European languages, morphed into the demonic opposite of a Christian "whiteness" and the Islamic "believer," and packaged into this crude and intellectually violent shorthand—"blackness"—were the pejorative ideas of Africans as barbarous, idolatrous, and without

---

⁹ Samuel Crowther, *Journal of an Expedition up the Niger and Tshadda rivers undertaken by Macgregor Laird in Connection with the British Government in 1854* (London: Church Missionary House, 1855), 228.

¹⁰ Ignatius Sancho, *Letters of the Late Ignatius Sancho, An African* . . . (London: J. Nichols, 1782), I: 82, II: 137, 155 (emphasis added).

¹¹ Nicholas Said, Th*e Autobiography of Nicholas Said, A Native of Bournou, Eastern Soudan, Central Africa* (Memphis, Tenn.: Shotwell & Co., 1873), 48–49 (emphasis added).

beauty and intelligence. Identity became a matter of racialized identification, and as indigenous African cultures and spiritualities were
targeted as the source of cultural identity and the source of the
difference between its bearers and European-Muslim slavers, both
culture and spirituality received the greatest amount of attention,
disdain, and vilification in the written accounts of enslavers and the
enslaved.

AFRICAN UNDERSTANDINGS OF RELIGION AND RETURN

Nowhere do we find the captive Africans' foundational self-understandings—as windows into their and their society's composite cultural
identity—more than in African cosmologies. These cosmologies were
often translated into social practice but more compellingly into indigenous spiritual practices through integral rituals, core ideas, dress,
ornamentation, scarification, therapeutics, ecological care, and culturally appropriate behaviors. By "spiritual" we mean "the conception of a
sacred cosmos that transcends physical reality in terms of significance
and meaning," and thus "spirituality" allows "us to apprehend the
sacred in our natural, ordinary surroundings," whereas the "religious"
refers to the "formalization of ritual, dogma, and belief, leading to a
systematic statement of syntactically suprarational tenets that may or
may not issue from a spiritual conception of the universe."[12] Thus, religion as institutionalized dogma and belief does not presuppose a culture in which it is rooted in the sense that, for instance, any Akan can
also be a Muslim, Buddhist, or Christian, but not any Muslim, Buddhist,
or Christian can become an Akan—birth through an Akan mother is
the foremost prerequisite for cultural identity and authentication. In
the documentary record, the most consistent spectacle of awe and
recoil for European governors, merchants, clergymen, and ship captain and crew alike were what they considered African "religions" or,
worse yet, "superstitions" and "heathenish beliefs." Islamic parallels
were not far away.

The phenomenon of transatlantic slaving was an occasion that
drew into its orbit a set of religious encounters and conflicts between
Christian, Islamic, and indigenous African spiritual adherents and of
those shuffling between all three. The Portuguese expulsion of their

---

[12] Marimba Ani, *Yurugu* (Trenton, N.J.: Africa World Press, 1994), 274.

Muslim overloads and the later Christian retaking of the Iberian Peninsula set in motion early transatlantic slaving at a time when Islamic communities began to take root in Sudanic Africa (i.e., west to east Africa at 12° to 32° north of the equator). These comparatively small communities with influence restricted to some non- or nominally Muslim political elites and polities remained largely that way, excluding the Swahili coast, until the eighteenth- and nineteenth-century jihadist movements. During the transatlantic era, both Islamic and anti-Islamic forces at times resisted and at times collaborated with Christian European merchants. Whereas significant forms of Christianity existed only in the northeast African corridor, the Kingdom of Kôngo and then the Angola region incrementally and varyingly fell under the spell of Catholicism in the sixteenth and seventeenth centuries. But even in these places, conversion occurred among the political elites, forced and mass baptism was common practice by Portuguese clergy for the newly enslaved, and resistance to Catholicism was significant among the general populace. Eurasian religions such as Islam and variants of Christianity in west and west central Africa was practiced not by the vast majority of Atlantic Africa, and forms of religious practice varied among those who partook in or rejected these religions.

Transatlantic Slaving as a Set of Religious Encounters

Even though much of the Africa associated with the transatlantic slave system adhered to indigenous spiritual/cultural practices and ideas—even for those who "converted" to Islam or Catholicism—they did engage with largely Christian merchants and clergymen and Islamized Africans and Arab Muslims who, in agreement with their European counterparts, viewed indigenous Africans as "unbelieving pagans" and "barbarians." That engagement has made for a sharp imbalance in the documentation: indigenous spiritualities receive scant and often disparaging treatment, there is a disproportionate number of enslaved African Muslim narratives relative to their actual numbers in western Africa, and (formerly enslaved) African Christians almost unanimously recalled their indigenous cultures and spiritualities with certain displeasures, while adhering to a missionary template where salvation triumphed over an "African" past of war and enslavement. In spite of these challenges, however, the available African narratives of enslavement for those who (almost) crossed the Atlantic and for those who stayed within Africa provide some important insights into African societies at the time of transatlantic slaving and its broader commercial and ideological reach into—and collaboration with—Islamic parts of Africa. Regardless of whether the predators differed in religious ideology, the common prey were often the non-Muslim, non-Christian, and nonelite people. But if this was a general pattern, the boundary between it and the exception was often crossed, almost erasing the age, wealth, rank, status, and religious orientation of the recorded 2 million captive Africans in the seventeenth century, the 6.5 million in the eighteenth century, and the 4 million in the nineteenth century who were evicted from their homelands.

§

Around 1725, Ukawsaw Gronniosaw (James Albert) of Borno was exported from the Gold Coast on board a Dutch slave ship. It appears he was a Muslim, based on his account of an Islamic prayer and his use of the possessive pronouns, "our" and "we": "One Saturday, (which is the day on which we keep our Sabbath) I labored under anxieties and fears that cannot be expressed. . . . I rose, as our custom is, about three o'clock, (as we are oblig'd to be at our place of worship an hour before the sun rise) we say nothing in our worship, but continue on our knees with our hands held up, observing a strict silence 'till the sun is at a certain height, which I suppose to be about 10 or 11 o'clock in England: when, at a certain sign made by the priest, we get up (our duty being over) and disperse to our different houses." Mahommah Baquaqua of Borgu shared an almost identical description, wherein his Muslim father "rose every morning at four o'clock for prayers, after which he returned to bed, at sunrise he performed his second devotional exercises, at noon he worshipped again, and again at sunset." Ukawsaw's familiarity with or curiosity about prayer would soon play a central part in an encounter with the ship's captain. En route to the Americas, the 15-year-old, who began his account describing his family and claiming "royal" pedigree in Borno, details a significant religious encounter, tempered by his age and Muslim background, between him and the Dutch ship captain. Ukawsaw had this to say about the encounter:

> After I had been a little while with my new master I grew more familiar, and ask'd him the meaning of prayer: (I could hardly speak English to be understood) he took great pains with me, and made me understand that he pray'd to God, who liv'd in Heaven; that He was my Father and Best Friend. I told him that this must be a

mistake; that my father liv'd at Bournou [Borno], and I wanted very much to see him, and likewise my dear mother, and sister, and I wish'd he would be so good as to send me home to them; and I added, all I could think of to induce him to convey me back.[13]

Supposing the Dutch captain spoke English as well and that Ukawsaw understood enough to have a conversation, the encounter reveals another story. If Ukawsaw, like Mahommah, was a dispassionate or nominal Muslim, which seems to be case from his fuller account, then he would have known something about prayer in Borno and its meaning in Islam and in non-Muslim spiritual practice and would have—via Islam—accepted notions of "God" and "Heaven." But when the Dutch captain translated the protestant "God" as Ukawsaw's "Father and Best Friend," Ukawsaw rejected this anthropomorphic idea of "God" ("this must be a mistake") and rightfully interpreted this phrase in the idiom of kin. "[M]y father liv'd at Bournou," Ukawsaw protested, "I wanted very much to see him, and likewise my dear mother, and sister, and I wish'd he would be so good as to *send me home to them*." From this dialogue, two central ideas emerge. First, what was an attempt to proselytize opened a moment of remembrance that ignited an argument for a return home—"and I added, all I could think of to induce him to convey me back." Second, Ukawsaw's language(s) and his exposure to indigenous spiritualities, even if he was reared in a Muslim family, would have interpreted the "gendering" and anthropomorphic rending of "God" as "He" and "Father" as foreign, and, consequently, he rejected the Dutch ship captain's theological argument as "a mistake." Ironically, in the end, Ukawsaw became a Baptist minister while in England decades after separation from his family.

During the transatlantic era, religious encounters and contestations also occurred within African societies and reveal to us much about the workings of those societies. More than a century after Ukawsaw left Borno and the Gold Coast, so too would another Muslim from Borno become enslaved and relate his account. But he, Mohammed Ali ben Said, spent much of his captivity in Africa, not the Americas. In a significant proportion of his account, Mohammed focuses on the encounters between Islam and indigenous spiritualities in Borno as well as the wider Sudanic region. In one instance he describes a benign

---

[13] James Albert Ukawsaw Gronniosaw, *A Narrative of the Most Remarkable Particulars in the Life of James Albert Ukawsaw Gronniosaw, an African Prince, as Related by Himself* (Bath, U.K.: W. Gye, 1770), 12.

form of Islam where "the King of Bornou [Borno], under whose reign [the] Molgoÿ became subservient to Bornou, granted the Molgoyans the free exercise of their religion, which was fetish, without human sacrifices. This fiendish practice is looked upon with abomination by all the nations and tribes of Soudan, both Mohammedan and pagan." Though, in the Qur'an, Allah commands a willing Abraham (Ibrahim) to sacrifice his first and dear son, Ishmael, it seems that this instance of "human sacrifice" was not inspired by Islam and that the practice, if any, was extremely limited given the widespread opposition to it by both Islamic and non-Islamic peoples. And though some might question why an Islamic ruler would sanction "the free exercise of [a] religion" rooted in "fetish" (read: non-Islamic belief), this move might have been indicative of the co-existence between non-Muslims and Muslims, some of whom were not fervent jihadists. This interpretation also falls in line with Mohammed's own view of the Sudan before Islam and the destruction left in the wake of its encounter with indigenous cultures. His perspective is worth quoting at length:

That previous to the introduction of Islamism in Soudan arts and sciences had reached a respectable attitude is attested by the ruins of several towns in Bornou, Mariadi, Nouffi and other countries. The ruins of Gambarou, the Bisnia of geographers, covers an immense area, the walls of which were built of burnt clay, extensive palaces, gardens, and other works of art flourished. . . . I am unable to give the slightest idea as to the time when Mohammedanism was introduced into Central Africa. But be it as it may, it brought with it desolation and ruin.

Anything like enterprise was rendered impossible, fanaticism and bigotry overruled everything, and the *Mohammed proselytes at once arrayed themselves against every non-follower of the Prophet as his implacable enemies.* Crusade after crusade was made against the pagan tribes, who, if they had the misfortune to fall into the hands of the Moslems, were either massacred or reduced into slavery. Cities after cities were razed to the ground.

The last thing of the kind took place toward the first part of this [nineteenth] century, when Othman Danfodio [Usman dan Fodio], a Fellatah [Fula(ni)] Chief, arrogated to himself the title of a prophet, saying that Allah (God) prescribed him to make war on all the Pagan nations of Central Africa, and promised him victory. The Fellatahs, who were then dispersed over the whole of Soudan, and who led a pastoral and nomadic life, under petty Chiefs, were collected by him under his sway. After several years of preparation, Danfodio, who had by this time a complete control over his countrymen, raised a formidable army of one hundred and eighty thousand warriors, and immediately assailed Houssa [Hausa], which was readily subjugated. Kano, the capital of Houssa, was consumed into ashes, *thousands of its male population were put to the sword, and the women and children were carried into slavery.* After committing other unheard of cruelties, Danfodio invaded successively and successfully, Gouber, Mariadi, Zeg-Zeg, Kârè Kârè, lastly Bornou which was then the preponderating power in Soudan. After two years of manly resistance, Bornou was compelled by force of arms to submit to the yoke of the Fellatahs. Our cities were destroyed, *thousands upon thousands were sold to the coast into bondage,* and many more were sold to the Barbary States. After two more years of humiliation the inhabitants of Bornou, under El Kanemy [Muhammad al-Amin al-Kanemi], revolted against our oppressors, and, in less time than a year, the Fellatahs were completely driven out of our country.[14]

Perhaps that marauding group that captured Mohammed and sent him on an enslaved and later indentured journey across five continents was Fula(ni). Be that as it may, we know with more certainty that around 1867, while in Europe, Mohammed, like his fellow "countryman" Ukawsaw, "had an irresistible desire to visit my native country. I at first tried to overcome that feeling but all in vain. . . . When I communicated my wishes to the [Russian] Prince [Nicholas Vassilievitch Troubetzkoy, to whom Mohammed was indentured] he tried to ridicule me, stating that I was no longer an African but a citizen of Europe. He said I could not reconcile myself to the manners and customs of my countrymen. . . . All this, however, did not deter me from returning to Soudan."[15] Mohammad, however, would convert to orthodox Christianity and assume a slightly new name – Nicholas Said. While, oddly enough, at "the 'Strangers' Home for Asiatics, Africans, and South Sea Islanders,' located on the West India Dock," Mohammed tells us his "fondness for travel asserted its supremacy," and instead of returning home he chose the Americas and to go with an employer who would defraud him out of his money while there.

It is possible that Mohammed Said's perspectives on the encounters between Islam and non-Muslim peoples in Sudanic Africa was shaped by his later conversion to Christianity, which he initially resisted at the demand of his holder, but this seems less likely for someone so learned and well traveled and who reflected the nature of Islamic practice among nonelites in Borno and elsewhere. Viewed from the perspective of Mohammed's experiences, the number of enslaved African Muslims who crossed the Atlantic or the Sahara and converted to Christianity should not be surprising at all. They were,

---

[14] Said, *Autobiography*, 10, 15–17 (emphasis added).
[15] Ibid., 185–86.

FIGURE 3   Slave market in Islamic Egypt, ca. 1830. (French School, (19th century) / Bibliotheque des Arts Decoratifs, Paris, France / Archives Charmet / The Bridgeman Art Library.)

after all, domiciled in Christian societies as enslaved or indentured individuals, and they were likely exported from their homelands at the hands of other Muslims. Between the eighteenth and twentieth centuries, African Muslims such as Ayuba Suleiman Diallo of Bundu, Ali Eisami Gazirambe and Mohammed Said of Borno, Salih Bilali of Masina, Mahommah Baquaqua of Borgu, Lahman Kibby (Kebe) and Abdul Rahman Ibrahima of Futa Jallon, Omar bin Said of Futa Toro, Abu Bakr al-Siddiq and Fatma Barka of Timbuktu, and Dada Masiti of

Brava (Somalia) were either captured by or sold to fellow Muslims, though the majority ended up among Christians. But not all of these individuals converted, nominally or otherwise, to Christianity, and so the question is what explains their varied religious responses to a shared condition of enslavement and Christian ideology? One view is offered by Mahommah Baquaqua, who described Ramadan ("a great fast . . . which lasts a month") as "the worship of the false prophet" on one hand, but saw "Africans [as] a superstitious race of people, [who] believe[d] in witchcraft and other supernatural agencies."[16] This view is significant, for it demonstrates at least two key points. First, Islamization in African societies and families was not a singular or totalizing phenomenon, and Mahommah's parents underscore this reality: "His father was Mahommedan in religion, but his mother was of no religion at all [read: non-Muslim]. . . . She liked Mahommedanism very well, but did not care much about the worshipping part of the matter." Second, if "Africans are a superstitious *race* of people," then the supposition is the Muslims are *not* Africans, for conversion signaled a rupture with the "African" past, and, thus, those many unconverted souls in Africa were "considered by the Mahommedans as a very *wicked* people." Now, it is certainly plausible that Mahommah's views, like those of Mohammed Said, were shaped by his conversion to Christianity, but this also seems improbable because Mahommah was abandoning his Islamic belief or the practice of his family *before* leaving Africa, as evidenced by his repeated escapes from the rigors of Qur'anic schooling and his acute drunkenness. His indifference and later rejection of Islam provides another important perspective on the nature of religious practice and religion as a source of identity in Africa and on the religious encounters within and beyond the shores of this continent.[17]

What Mahommah's story also tells us is that encounters with and a conversion to Christianity was not a matter of salvation, but rather a means to specific goals. After his conversion, he "gave up drinking and all other kinds of vices," for it was drunkenness that led to his capture and eventual exportation from his homeland. Second, he saw the financial support offered by those who orchestrated his conversion— and their access to potential funders of the same faith—as a way to return home, so as long as he could convince his Christian backers that, upon his return, he would "preach the Gospel of glad tidings of great joy to the ignorant and benighted of my fellow countrymen who are now believers in the false prophet Mahomed." If indeed Mahommah

---

[16] Baquaqua, *Biography*, 22.
[17] Ibid., 23, 26.

had a dream of returning to Africa the night before his conversion, then he might have enlisted as a Christian missionary to get back to Africa. Abdul Rahman of Timbo, Futa Jallon, and Natchez, Mississippi, had done so with the same expectations from his Christian backers, but he did not make it back to Timbo nor did he relinquish his faith. Even if Mahommah converted to Christianity with pure sincerity, there was much in Islam he would have seen in (Baptist) Christianity more than the Roman Catholicism he experienced while enslaved in Brazil, on which he noted, "we were taught to chant some words which we did not know the meaning of," referring to its paraphernalia as "images of clay" [read: idolatry] under which he and other enslaved individuals had to kneel and the crucifix as a "wooden god." Of course, Mahommah would have read these rituals and their paraphernalia as he had interpreted indigenous African spiritualities: the work of "witchcraft and other supernatural agencies" and officiators who muttered the unintelligible language of "astrologer[s]" and "medicine men." But the accounts of other enslaved Africans from Sudanic Africa indicate what Mahommah labeled "astrologers," who "consult[ed] the stars, and by that means trace out the supposed witch," interwove "the[ir] religion [of] Paganism," according to another Muslim Selim Aga, "with several Mahommedan rites, such as the shaving of their heads, circumcision, and fasting." If we discard the Islamic bias, then we can draw two conclusions with greater veracity. First, the search for "witches" was a hunt for antisocial forces, human and otherwise, in order to maintain social order, as members of society saw fit. In the largest African slaving region of west central Africa, the idiom of "witchcraft," understood in local terms, was strongly associated with greed, wrongful accumulation, and transatlantic slaving.[18] Second, there were areas of agreement between Islam and indigenous cultures, for the shaving of heads, circumcision, and fasting were not unique to Islam, and all three rituals have a long tenure in non-Islamic parts of Africa. In effect, humans tend to be more receptive to commonalities or what complements existing practices if they see a benefit and no threat to their foundational self-understandings from an adoptable idea, ritual, or practice.

The eighteenth- and nineteenth-century religious worlds of Mahommah from Borgu and Selim from the Sudan were, thematically, no different than that of Olaudah Equiano from Igboland and

---

[18] See John K. Thornton, "Cannibals, Witches and Slave Traders in the Atlantic World," *William and Mary Quarterly* 60, no. 2 (2003): 273–94.

Joseph Wright from Egbaland. For Equiano, writing some 32 years after his departure from Igboland and as a Christian, he recalled the following about the indigenous spiritual practices of his homeland:

> As to religion, the natives believe that there is one Creator of all things, and that *he* lives in the sun, and is girted round with a belt that he may never eat or drink; but, according to some, *he* smokes a pipe, which is our own favorite luxury. They believe *he* governs events, especially our deaths or captivity; but, as for the doctrine of eternity, I do not remember to have ever heard of it: some however believe in the transmigration of souls in a certain degree. Those spirits, which are not transmigrated, such as our dear friends or relations, they believe always attend them, and guard them from the bad spirits or their foes. For this reason they always before eating, as I have observed, put some small portion of the meat, and pour some of their drink, on the ground for them; and they often make oblations of the blood of beasts or fowls at their graves. I was very fond of my mother, and almost constantly with her. When she went to make these oblations at her mother's tomb, which was a kind of small solitary thatched house, I sometimes attended her. There she made her libations, and spent most of the night in cries and lamentations.[19]

We will come back to Equiano in a moment, because we need to pause to digest a few salient points made in the above description. First, a transformation has occurred on two levels: Equiano used the *masculine* subject pronoun "he" to talk about a "Creator of all things," when the Igbo language did not draw "gender" distinction in the use of subject pronouns, and this gender-neutral "Creator" now possessed a masculine gender—as in the Christian "our father"—and became anthropomorphic, like the Greek "gods," with human appetites and desires. We are not suggesting this transformation started with Equiano, but certainly from the eighteenth century into the present, the "gendered" and "demonic" language used to interpret African spiritualities and their practitioners has been a Christian one, through whose optic those spiritualities became the function of "gods," "devils," "witches," and "bad spirits." In spite of the religio-linguistic trappings found in English for the "Igbo" speaker, Equiano went on to make a larger, more fundamental point about the spirituality he and his mother engaged:

> This necessary habit of decency was with us a part of religion, and therefore we had many purifications and washings; indeed almost as many, and used on the same

---

19 Equiano, *Interesting Narrative*, 27–29.

occasions, if my recollection does not fail me, as the Jews. Those that touched the dead at any time were obliged to wash and purify themselves before they could enter a dwelling-house. Every woman too, at certain times, was forbidden to come into a dwelling-house, or touch any person, or anything we ate . . . till offering was made, and then we were purified.

Though we had no places of public worship, we had priests and magicians, or wise men . . . [who] were held in great reverence by the people. They calculated our time, and foretold events. . . . These magicians were also our doctors or physicians. They practiced bleeding by cupping; and were very successful in healing wounds and expelling poisons. They had likewise some extraordinary method of discovering jealously, theft, and poisoning; the success of which no doubt they derived from their unbounded influence over the credulity and superstition of the people.[20]

If we ignore the last clause, which can be read as Equiano's Christian rather than his cultural lens, it should be clear from the above that culture was "religion" and "religion" was culture. One of the most enduring and, at times, self-imposed challenge for those who look for African "religion" is not that it does not exist or that it exists but is difficult to find. Rather, African "religion" had no name (to the outsider or converted insider) because it was not a *separate* realm of life. Hence, when Equiano talked about "decency" and "religion" as separate matters that could and did co-exist in Igbo society, he was a prisoner of the language he used and the religion he now claimed, because the language of religion presupposes a detachable "religion" that could be claimed by any culture, whereas the converse would not be true for a culture. What one does to purify and why, how one treats the dead and the living, how one cares for the physical and immaterial illnesses of society, uncovering jealousy and theft and providing a sense of security and belonging all formed a composite culture that did (and does) not require a "religion" in order to be. But for some enslaved and later Christianized Africans, such as Joseph Wright, who relied on the spiritual technologies of his culture to provide security, the tide of intra-group warfare and famine created immense vulnerabilities and led to his eventual capture and enslavement. When he was around 10 years old, war came upon Joseph and his "respectable parents" and siblings; this war was "not by another nation," but rather his own—"we all one nation speaking one language." The warfare and famine drove his parents and others to seek food elsewhere. In their absence, the children and those left behind sought divine intervention

---

[20] Ibid., 31–34.

by "sacrificing to our gods. There is a god which we call public god . . . and the name of that god was Borowah. *To this we all looking for help* . . . [and through the] thousands of private gods the people keeping in their houses." Despite the Christian optics filtering Joseph's account, what we see is recourse to spiritual tools that could help and thus their widespread presence in many homes. After the city walls were besieged and the locality was in "sorrowful silence," we can imagine how Joseph and others might be have lost faith in the so-called "gods," especially after the "chief priest" of Borowah, a "very dear relation" to Joseph's father, committed suicide. Joseph and his siblings were captured, exchanged several times, reunited and then separated from kin, and "brought to white Portuguese [men] for sale, [and] after strict examination the white man put me and some [of the] other[s] aside." British naval intervention would rescue him from an Atlantic crossing, and Joseph would actually return to what was left of his family in Abeokuta as a Christianity missionary.[21] Joseph penned his life story in June 1839, and by then some 3.5 million captive Africans were not rescued but rather transported to the Americas by the "Christian" nation of England. Each of these persons evicted from his or her homeland carried a composite culture across the Atlantic, and we have some sense of the encounter between such cultures—carried in the minds and accumulated memory of the enslaved—and the new environments and religions of the Americas.

Religion and Return in the Transatlantic Era

In North America, where the smallest number of Africans disembarked but where we find the largest volume of "slave narratives," second- or third-generation Africans of the diaspora, such as Charles Ball, have much to teach us about the transfer and use of composite African cultures across the Atlantic. Charles published his now-famous 517-page narrative two years before Joseph Wright penned his, and both, as we shall see shortly, provide important perspectives on notions of religion and return in the transatlantic era. Charles, an enslaved person with later fugitive status, had traveled from Maryland, his state of birth, to South Carolina and Georgia and had made considerable observations, tempered by his status and relative

---

[21] "The Life of Joseph Wright, A Native of Ackoo," Wesleyan Methodist Missionary Society Archive, Special Collections, Library of the School of Oriental and African Studies (London), West Africa Correspondence, Sierra Leone, 1839, Box 280, pp. 1–4, 7, 9–10, 17–20.

mobility. Traveling in the heartland of the U.S. South, he was therefore in a key position to observe and comment on the spiritualities of the "great many African slaves in the country." Charles "became intimately acquainted with some of these men. Many of them believed there were several gods; some of whom were good, and others evil, and they prayed as much to the latter as to the former. I knew several who must have been, from what I have since learned, Mohamedans [Muslims]; though at that time, I had never heard of the religion of Mohamed." Charles used the language of the Christian religion and its lens to describe those who inhabited a universe of "several gods" of "good" and "evil" character. What Charles could have understood but failed to appreciate is that the "Creator" (in Equiano's words) as a force was too vast for the human mind to fully comprehend, but could be parceled out in specific locales in nature (e.g., sacred rivers, mountains, forests) and as accessible yet manageable forces more immediate to human life. These manageable forces were then domesticated by human culture and could be experienced through a range of knowledge systems—divination, so-called trance and possession—and petitioned through libation and sacrifices, with the meaning of "acting sacred toward."[22] Thus, what Charles called "gods," unfortunately but understandably, were in fact those manifold expressions of the "Creator" force that functioned as tools, which, of course, could be used for "good" and "evil" ends. The issue here are not the tools (or so-called "gods"), but rather what one does with the tools, in the same way that a hammer could help to build or destroy a house.[23]

Guided by his Christian reading, which viewed the African's "religion" as its demonic inverse, Charles concluded, "There is, in general, very little sense of religious obligation, or duty, amongst the slaves on the cotton plantations; and *Christianity cannot be, with propriety, called the religion of these people.* They are universally subject to the grossest and most abject superstition; and uniformly believe in witchcraft, conjuration, and the agency of evil spirits in the affairs of human life. Far the greater part of them are either natives of Africa, or the descendants of those who have always, from generation to generation,

---

[22] On the transmission of historical and spiritual knowledge through "spirit possession," see Richard Price, *Travels with Tooy: History, Memory, and the African American Imagination* (Chicago: University of Chicago Press, 2008), 38.

[23] Charles Ball, *Slavery in the United States: A Narrative of the Life and Adventures of Charles Ball, a Black Man, Who Lived Forty Years in Maryland, South Carolina and Georgia, as a Slave Under Various Masters, and was One Year in the Navy with Commodore Barney, During the Late War* (New York: John S. Taylor, 1837), 164–65.

lived in the south, since their ancestors were landed on this continent; and *their superstition . . . does not deserve the name of religion.*" If Charles is accurate, and the historical records seem to agree, large numbers of African descendants in the early nineteenth century were far from being Christians, especially in the traditional U.S. South. But, in Charles's observations, Africans were not simply evicted from their homelands but evicted from humanity and a human culture and spirituality, for their "abject superstition," uniform "belie[f] in witchcraft, conjuration, and the agency of evil spirits" disqualified them. Once disqualified from humanity, the "native Africans" could be nothing more than "revengeful, and unforgiving in their tempers, easily provoked, and cruel in their designs." Those like Charles even despised the "native Africans" because they "discover[ed] no beauty in the fair complexions, and delicate forms of their [white] mistresses" and because they felt "indignant at the servitude that is imposed upon them, and only want power to inflict the most cruel retribution upon their oppressors." Since Charles's "grandfather was brought from Africa," and he knew something about him, what would the elder "native African" have thought about his grandson's characterization of people like him? What ideas might the grandfather have shared with Charles? In the end, Charles was convinced that the "natives of Africa, or the descendants of those who have always, from generation to generation, lived in the south," were "universally of opinion, and this opinion is founded in their religion, that after death they shall return to their own country, and rejoin their former companions and friends, in some happy region."[24]

The idea of returning to one's "own country" is ubiquitous in the literature of the African diaspora and remains a source of contention for those who argue for a continuity of culture between Africa and the Americas, a disruption in this flow and the creation of a new culture, or an intermediary position somewhere in between. In Stephanie E. Smallwood's *Saltwater Slavery: A Middle Passage from Africa to American Diaspora*, Charles Ball is quoted from another source as recalling an "African-born slave's funerary ritual" in which a man "decorated the grave of his departed son with a miniature canoe, about a foot long, and a little paddle, with which he said it would cross the ocean to his own country." Smallwood then claimed, "This man's ritual mortuary practice *would not have held any meaning for his kin and community in Africa.* None had been required to travel a distance so great and so perilous to reach the realm of the ancestors, and

---

[24] Ibid., 165, 219 (emphasis added).

none had required the assistance of a canoe and paddle to achieve the soul's departure for another realm. *It was a gesture that could be understood only by those who shared the memory of the slave ship.*" This claim, of course, is part of larger argument, reverberating throughout the Americas, and it goes something like this: "The cultures they [the enslaved] produced do not reflect the simple transfer and continuation of Africa in the Americas but rather reflect the elaboration of specific cultural content and its transformation to meet the particular needs of slave life in the Atlantic system. . . . In this sense, the cultural practices of diasporic Africa could have meaning only outside Africa."[25] While there is much to appreciate in Smallwood's argument and while her reading of the funerary ritual might seem novel, in fact there is much that is equally a gross misreading of the ritual and its implications for the question of African culture and spirituality as shaped by transatlantic slavery.

The above argument is both a misreading of the particular evidence used and a misleading general conclusion drawn. In Charles Ball's 1837 narrative, he begins with the father of the deceased child, the officiant of the funerary ritual and whom Charles described as "a native of a country far in the interior of Africa, [who] said he had been a priest in his own nation." The identity and competencies of this unnamed father is central to our reinterpretation. "A few days before Christmas," Charles continued

> [the] child died, after an illness of only three days. I assisted her and her husband to inter the infant – which was a little boy – and its father buried with it, *a small bow, and several arrows; a little bag of parched meal; a miniature canoe, about a foot long, and a little paddle,* (with which he said it would *cross the ocean to his own country)* a small *stick,* with an iron nail, sharpened, and fastened into one end of it; and a *piece of white muslin,* with *several curious and strange figures painted on it in blue and red,* by which, he said, *his relations and countrymen would know the infant to be his son,* and would receive it accordingly, on its arrival amongst them.[26]

Since South Carolina, the locus of this ritual, had a significant Akan presence from the Gold Coast of West Africa—the region of Smallwood's study where the Akan were (and are) the cultural nucleus—it is

---

[25] Stephanie E. Smallwood, *Saltwater Slavery: A Middle Passage from Africa to American Diaspora* (Cambridge, Mass.: Harvard University Press, 2007), 189–90; W. Jeffrey. Bolster, *Black Jacks: African American Seamen in the Age of Sail* (Cambridge, Mass.: Harvard University Press, 1998), 49; Ball, *Slavery,* 264–65.

[26] Ball, *Slavery,* 264–65 (emphasis added).

more than probable that the "priest" in question originated there. Fortunately for us, Charles left us with specific cultural details (italicized above) that, when added to eyewitness accounts of merchants who knew the Gold Coast and the slaving enterprise that brought many Akan culture bearers to the Americas, lead us to a different set of conclusions.[27] We know the range of implements used in the ritual—bow and arrow, cornmeal, canoe and paddle, stick with nail, white cloth, and "several curious and strange figures"—but we do not know why those items and for what ends. The Lutheran pastor W. J. Müller, stationed among the seafaring peoples of the Gold Coast between 1662 and 1669, observed that Akan peoples in their homeland "believed that man's soul . . . is immortal" and, after physical death, "they come to a wonderful country." Kinfolks would "approach the deceased and ask what was the cause of his dying, and whether he lacked food and drink." The prepared grave was "only dug at 4 or 5 foot deep, and when the corpse has been coveted with earth, a square mud table is erected over the grave. On it are placed the *tools* with which the deceased earned his living in this life, as well as what he needs for daily domestic use. In particular it is on no account forgotten to place large pots of palm wine, dishes of *milie* [Turkish corn or wheat], palm oil and all kinds of local fruits on the grave, so that the deceased may lack neither food nor drink. . . . They also make *male and female figures out of clay and paint them red and white*. These are supposed to represent the deceased." A decade later, French merchant and slaver Jean Barbot wrote, "The priests, or conjurers, are generally their physicians and surgeons, as well as spiritual guides," and though sometimes the Akan peoples use a "wooden coffin" or "bury their dead in a sea chest . . . [about] four foot, or four foot and a half in length," these peoples "commonly lay their dead in graves about four foot deep, and having placed the body there in, with the board it is fastened to, they cover it with as many green boughs, or other things, as will serve to bear off the earth, and *bury with it the arms, clothes and utensils, the deceased person used while living*; together with the *new idols, made by the priest*." Why do all this for the deceased? Using Gold Coast informants, Barbot responded, "most believe that immediately after death, they go to another world, where they live off the offerings of provisions, money and clothes, their relations left behind make for them after their decease. . . . [T]he dead are conveyed to a famous river . . .

---

[27] On the Akan in South Carolina, see Kwasi Konadu, *The Akan Diaspora in the Americas* (New York: Oxford University Press, 2010), esp. chap. 6.

[where] their god enquires into their past life, whether they have religiously observ'd their festival or sabbath, and whether they have inviolably abstained from all forbidden meats, and kept their oaths? If so, *they are gently wasted over that river into a country where there is nothing but happiness*; but, if they have, on the contrary, transgressed those observances, the deity plunges them into the river, where they are drowned and buried in perpetual oblivion."[28] The departed son would have taken the former path and would have been well served by the tools of manhood ("a small bow, and several arrows" and "a small stick, with an iron nail"), tools for his likely trade as fisherman and for the journey home ("a miniature canoe . . . and a little paddle"), food for the journey ("a little bag of parched meal"), and protective symbols or figures ("white muslin, with several curious and strange figures painted on it in blue and red") coded in a language that "his relations and country-men would know."

Charles's recollection and Müller and Barbot's observations undermine Smallwood's interpretation and make it quite clear that (1) the funerary ritual would have resonated deeply with the priest-father's kin and community in Africa and would not have presupposed a shared "memory of the slave ship"; (2) since no one has traveled to and from the "realm of the ancestors," we do not know enough about the distance or its perils to know what is required or what is sufficient for the journey; and, lastly, (3) the nature of African culture and spiritual-ity in the Americas was about "transfer and continuation" *and* the "elaboration [or transformation] of specific cultural content . . . to meet the particular [and general] needs" of those concerned, registering on certain frequencies more than others in "diasporic Africa" *and* within Africa. Ultimately, the most profound statement made by such rituals was the reconstitution of family – an argument we have made since the first chapter and one which, in this instance, is sustained by the evi-dence. The implications of this composite interpretation have at least two forms: one is pragmatic, the other spiritual (as defined earlier in this chapter). In a very real way, some enslaved Africans sought and acted upon the urge to physically return home. In one instance, a defi-ant Broteer (Venture Smith) told his holder, boldly, "I crossed the waters to come here and I am willing to cross them to return." In

[28] For Müller's account, see Adam Jones, *German Sources for West African History, 1599–1669* (Wiesbaden, Germany: Franz Steiner Verlag, 1983), 258; Jean Barbot, "A Description of the Coasts of North and South-Guinea," in Awnsham Churchill, *A Collection of Voyages and Travels . . .* (London: Messrs. Churchill, 1732), V: 282, 307.

another instance, a small group of Akan peoples in early nineteenth-century Jamaica "told some of their shipmates . . . they would proceed to the sea-side by night, and remain in the bush through the night, and the first canoe they found by the seaside they would set sail for their country."[29] At the level of spiritual culture even a condescending Charles Ball, who disparaged the "native Africans" and viewed the priest-father as "cruel," could not help "but respect the sentiments which inspired his affection for his child," once he (Charles) gathered a modicum of the meaning and purpose of the ritual he witnessed. In the end, Charles tells us, the priest-father "cut a lock of hair from his head, threw it upon the dead infant, and closed the grave with his own hands. He then told us the God of his country was looking at him, and was pleased with what he had done." The priest-father gave part of himself ("a lock of hair") as his ultimate gesture of sacrifice, bond, and mourning, for, in the Akan homeland, mourning was expressed by cutting or growing one's hair and by fasting several days from food or drinking, among other things. As a "priest," the child's father was well positioned to communicate the trans-Atlantic meaning of his spiritual culture with his "relations and countrymen" and "the God of his country" as well as to his wife Lydia, Charles Ball, and to us outside of Africa.

Not too long after the "funeral service" ended, "Lydia told [Charles] she was rejoiced that her child was dead, and out of a world in which slavery and wretchedness must have been its only portion. I am now, said she, ready to follow my child, and the sooner I go, the better for me. . . . When she [died] . . . I assisted in carrying her to the grave, which I closed upon her, and covered with green turf. She sleeps by the side of her infant, in a corner of the negro grave-yard, of this plantation."[30] It seems strange that the priest-father did not perform the same funerary ritual for his wife as he had done for their child and that Charles did not mention it. Could it be that Lydia was born in South Carolina and her husband or Charles did not view her as a "native African," or that Charles saw her as an "American Negro" who deserved (and probably received) a Christian burial? We have no sure answers to these questions, but Charles seem to have had a lot to do with these questions—it is his narrative and memory, after all. In sharp contrast with the so-called "native Africans," Charles argued, "The case is different with the

[29] Cited in Michael Mullin, *Africa in America: Slave Acculturation and Resistance in the American South and the British Caribbean, 1736–1831* (Urbana: University of Illinois Press, 1992), 14.
[30] Ball, *Slavery*, 266.

American negro, who knows nothing of Africa, her religion, or customs, and *who has borrowed all his ideas of present and future happiness, from the opinions and intercourse of white people, and of Christians.* He is, perhaps, not so impatient of slavery, and excessive labor, as the native of Congo; but his mind is bent upon other pursuits, and his discontent works out for itself other schemes, than those which agitate the brain of the imported negro. His heart pants for no heaven beyond the waves of the ocean." The argument Charles made is a familiar one: the American experience for the (formerly) enslaved trumped all others experiences, as the first waves of the enslaved were Christianized and Europeanized "Atlantic creoles" and the latter waves were essentially recast in the "borrowed" image of "white [Christian] people," hence notions of a "black" Christianity, a "black" church, a "black" community, and, stopping short of a longer list, a "black" people. The problem is that Charles's argument and its revival by contemporary writers is weakened by the voices of the enslaved themselves.

To be sure, the enslaved voices we have at our disposal paint a varied, resistive, and contradictory picture that questions their degree of Christianization or Catholicization, well into the late nineteenth century and, speculatively, into the twentieth century. Lunsford Lane (ca. 1803–1879) of North Carolina recalled, "Indeed I, with others, was often told by the minister how good God was in bringing us over to this country from dark and benighted Africa, and permitting us to listen to the sound of the gospel. To me, God also granted temporal freedom, which man without God's consent, had stolen away."[31] Lunsford's insights should not be missed: he questioned how "good" the Christian God was and thus how "dark and benighted Africa" really was, since he was robbed of his "temporal freedom" by enslaving Christians who preached two-facedness. This hypocrisy did not go unnoticed among the enslaved. In one poignant instance, an individual we know only as Aaron chastised "northern" abolitionists and ministers for their public support of "freedom" but private refusal to help the enslaved or newly emancipated as well as "southern" ministers for the vast chasm between their piety and enslaving practices. Aaron used this "great knowledge of the Bible" to make his case, but he "cannot read a word," demonstrating that rote memorization of

---

[31] Lunsford Lane, *The Narrative of Lunsford Lane, Formerly of Raleigh, N.C. Embracing an Account of His Early Life, the Redemption by Purchase of Himself and Family from Slavery, and His Banishment from the Place of His Birth for the Crime of Wearing a Colored Skin* (Boston: J. G. Torrey, 1842), 20.

theology cannot serve as evidence of conversion nor of an understanding of a theology.[32] As Mohammed Said observed of Islam in Sudanic Africa, for instance, "Before we went to the Malam we could repeat a great number of prayers, but like many Roman Catholics, who daily say 'Pater Noster' and 'Ave Maria,' we did not understand the meaning of one word."[33] Like Aaron, Thomas H. Jones (ca. 1806?–1885?) also hailed from North Carolina but was a literate preacher who, curiously, included in his narrative a fictional account of a "Wild Tom," perhaps his alter ego, who personified the tension between Christian evangelization among the "Wild Toms" and the omnipresent fear of backsliding. In the following passage, "Thomas" is "Wild Tom":

> Since the death of his wife [who was whipped to death by an overseer], *a remarkable change had taken place in my friend Thomas*. . . . I had abundant reason to suspect that *he had totally renounced the religion in which he had been so carefully instructed*; and which, for so long a time, had exercised so powerful an influence over him. *He had secretly returned to the practice of certain wild rites*, which in his early youth, he had learned from his mother, who had herself been kidnapped from the coast of Africa, and who had been, as he had often told me, zealously devoted to her country's superstitions. He would sometimes talk wildly and incoherently about having seen the spirit of his departed wife, and of some promise he had made to the apparition; and I was led to believe that he suffered under occasional fits of partial insanity.[34]

The belief that people were renouncing "the religion" and returning to "wild rites" from "the coast of Africa" was as strong, if not stronger, than the belief in white or black Christianity itself. More to the point, the sheer terror of enslavement—and its debt peonage transmutation—for the self or kin could always cause "a remarkable change," transforming believers into incredulous backsliders or convincing some that the spell of the "gospel" could be translated into some kind of freedom. John Joseph, an Asante (Akan) from the Gold Coast, "gazed at [his holder in New Orleans] with contempt and said [to him] . . . you may

---

[32] Aaron, *The Light and Truth of Slavery. Aaron's History* (Worcester, Mass.: Author, 1845), 1.

[33] Nicholas Said, *The Autobiography of Nicholas Said, A Native of Bournou, Eastern Soudan, Central Africa* (Memphis, Tenn.: Shotwell & Co., 1873), 38.

[34] Thomas H. Jones, *Experience and Personal Narrative of Uncle Tom Jones; Who Was for Forty Years a Slave. Also the Surprising Adventures of Wild Tom, of the Island Retreat, a Fugitive Negro from South Carolina* (Boston: H. B. Skinner, 1858), 29–30.

be wicked enough to sell my body, but thank God, it is not in the power of a master or auctioneer, to buy and sell my precious and immortal soul." This defiance soon dissipated with the experience of enslavement, and John, formerly named Jack Sambo, not only claimed a Christian ideology but used it gain entry to England where he became a "free man" and, for his emancipators, a vehicle "to communicate to his poor African brethren the true word of God" upon his "return to his native country."[35] Abdul Rahman Ibrahima skillfully pretended to be a Christian to fundraise for his family's freedom and was thus also seen as an instrument for Christian conversion, though among those in Islamic West Africa.

We do not know what became of John Joseph once in England, and Abdul Rahman made it to Liberia but died without his North American family still in bondage, and without reaching his family in Timbo, Futa Jallon. But in spite of the distinct and, at times, ambivalent meanings returning home held, the center of gravity remained family, wherever the enslaved found themselves. John Joseph wondered about his enslaved sister while in England, Abdul Rahman wrestled with being "free" in Liberia without his grand- and great-grandchildren, and family weighed heavy on Louis Asa-Asa and his ambivalence about returning home after British antislavery ships rescued him and others from an Atlantic crossing. Listen to Louis:

I am very happy to be in England, as far as I am very well; – but *I have no friend belonging to me*, but God, who will take care of me as he has done already. I am very glad I have come to England, to know who God is. *I should like much to see my friends again, but I do not now wish to go back to them*: for if I go back to my own country, I might be taken as a slave again. I would rather stay here, where I am free, than go back to my country to be sold. I shall stay in England as long as (please God) I shall live. I wish the King of England could know all I have told you. I wish it that he may see how cruelly we are used. *We had no king in our country, or he would have stop[ped] it.* I think the king of England might stop it, and this is why I wish him to know it all. I have heard say he is good; and if he is, he will stop it if he can. I am well off myself, for I am well taken care of, and have good bed and good clothes; but I wish my own people to be as comfortable.[36]

[35] John Joseph, *The Life and Sufferings of John Joseph, a Native of Ashantee, in Western Africa . . .* (Wellington, New Zealand: J. Greedy, 1848), 5, 8.
[36] Mary Prince, *The History of Mary Prince, a West Indian Slave. Related by Herself. With a Supplement by the Editor. To Which Is Added, the Narrative of Asa-Asa, a Captured African* (London: F. Westley and A. H. Davis, 1831), 43–44.

When Louis penned or dictated the above in London in 1831, the matter of returning home took on several forms in a world where the relationship between Europe, Africa, and the Americas had shifted yet again with a number of paradoxes. For one, central authority in African states, especially those that owed either their emergence or expansion to transatlantic slaving, began to collapse from the loss of Atlantic commerce and from under the weight of increased domestic slavery to meet the demands of industrializing Europe's so-called "legitimate trade," increased missionary and mercantile activity on the coast and in the interior of Africa, and increased jihadist movements in Islamic West Africa and ivory and enslaved production in East Africa. In effect, the declining presence of transatlantic slavery in nineteenth-century West Africa had the ironic effect of increasing international slaving in west central Africa and southeast Africa and in regional slaving regimes in East Africa. Second, individuals like Samuel Crowther and James Macaulay, both "liberated" Africans and members of the ill-fated 1841 Christian Mission Society expedition up the Niger River, were reunited with kinfolk in their homeland and, for James, with one of the very women who sent him into captivity![37] Finally, transatlantic slaving, before and after its abolition, was never the simple matter of "Africans selling Africans," as we have tried to make clear in this and the preceding chapters. Decades after the British abolition of international slaving in 1807, localized forms of capacity increased in Africa and in the Americas and placed greater stress on vulnerable populations, as many African states fought to consolidate their rule over conquered or subjugated peoples and to halt impending European territorial conquest. Transatlantic slaving had, in many ways, made a path for this period of conquest, but the wider impact on African and American societies is still being assessed. The next chapter seeks only to be a part of that process, since the story of transatlantic slaving, unlike a tremor, is a history without closure and with deep reverberations into the present.

---

[37] James Frederick Schön and Samuel Crowther, *Journals of the Rev. James Frederick Schön and Mr. Samuel Crowther: Who, Accompanied the Expedition up the Niger, in 1841, in Behalf of the Church Missionary Society* (London: Hatchard and Son, 1842), 210–11.

FURTHER READINGS

Amadiume, Ifi. *Male Daughters, Female Husbands: Gender and Sex in an African Society.* London: Zed Books, 1987.

Baum, Robert M. *Shrines of the Slave Trade: Diola Religion and Society in Precolonial Senegambia: Diola Religion and Society in Precolonial Senegambia.* New York: Oxford University Press, 1999.

Falola, Toyin, and Matt D. Childs, eds. *The Yoruba Diaspora in the Atlantic World.* Bloomington: Indiana University Press, 2004.

Gomez, Michael A. *Black Crescent: The Experience and Legacy of African Muslims in the Americas.* New York: Cambridge University Press, 2005.

Sweet, James H. *Domingos Álvares, African Healing, and the Intellectual History of the Atlantic World.* Chapel Hill: University of North Carolina Press, 2011.

Sweet, James H. *Recreating Africa: Culture, Kinship, and Religion in the African-Portuguese World, 1441–1770.* Chapel Hill: University of North Carolina Press, 2003.

The Endless Voyage of Cannibalism and Capitalism: African Understandings of the Impacts of Transatlantic Slaving and Abolitionism

We were told that the whites were cannibals, and all the slaves that they bought were for no other but culinary purposes.

—Mohammed Ali ben Said

This chapter weighs the central arguments of the previous chapters through the lens of African metaphors and cultural idioms in the nineteenth century, so as to offer a composite view of the ways in which Africans grappled with and are still, in many ways, interpreting the impact of transatlantic slaving on self, society, and the diasporas spawned by it. This chapter, like the previous ones, privileges enslaved African rather than scholarly interpretations—of which there are plenty. Such African interpretations are essential to a fuller understanding of the transatlantic slave system and its human consequences. To be sure, African readings of that system as an endless voyage of cannibalism and capitalism were widespread among the published voices and the voiceless, from Equiano, who wondered, "if we were not to be eaten by those white men with horrible looks, red faces, and loose hair," to José Monzolo of Kôngo, who said, in 1659, that Africans "believed that [those] whom they called whites, brought them to kill them and to make the flags for the ships from their remains, for when they were red it was from the blood of the Moors [Africans], and desperately fearing this many threw themselves in the sea."[1] These widespread beliefs of cannibalism among Africans from Senegambia to Southeast Africa were matched by similar beliefs among European and Arab Muslim slavers who, through their religious lenses, remained convinced that Africans were cannibals and pagans. In the Americas, white soldiers, planters, and politicians willfully accepted—with little effort, evidence, or experience in Africa—that "these poor pagans and (in many cases) cannibals from the coast of Africa" would only "cease to be cannibals and savages" by "Christian civilization" in ways akin to the "domestication of wild animals and fowls."[2] The Africans' presumed cannibalism and paganism calcified as a fixed truth during the transatlantic era and reified as the foremost character of "black" labor forces in colonial and postcolonial contexts.

For both slavers and the enslaved, there were also corresponding understandings of capitalist commodification as cannibalism. Even advocates of North American slavery such as George Fitzhugh (1806–1881) would argue, ironically, that "all good and respectable [white] people are 'Cannibals all,' who do not labor, or who are successfully trying to live without labor, on the unrequited labor of other people." Fitzhugh invoked cannibalism not based on enslaved African understandings but rather on his reckoning of capitalist commodification as

---

[1] Olaudah Equiano, *The Interesting Narrative of the Life of Olaudah Equiano, or Gustavus Vassa, the African* (London: Author, 1789), I: 72; cited in John Thornton, "Cannibals, Witches, and Slave Traders in the Atlantic World," *William and Mary Quarterly* 60, no. 2 (2003): 273.

[2] James B. Avirett, *The Old Plantation: How We Lived in Great House and Cabin before the War* (New York: F. Tennyson Neely Co., 1901), 14; John Allan Wyeth, *With Sabre and Scalpel: The Autobiography of a Soldier and Surgeon* (New York: Harper & Brothers Publishers, 1914), 10.

a powerful, cannibalizing force among the (former) planters and merchants—the "vampire capitalist class"—who amassed their plots of land and possessions with captive labor.[3] But some Africans acutely understood that they and the sheer violence they encountered were central to transatlantic slaving and the rise and movement of global capitalism, which created capital in a gold- and silver-based capitalist economy by transforming captive Africans into precious metals. Indeed, slave ship captains were duly instructed to "turn your whole Cargoe of Goods and Negroes into Gold," for these Africans were "a perishable commodity," and, as Daniel Defoe noted in 1713, "no African trade, no negroes; no negroes no sugars, gingers, indicoes [sic], etc; no sugars etc no islands, no islands no continent; no continent no trade."[4] African merchants and mercenaries involved in transatlantic slaving depended on credit extended from Atlantic commerce, since guns, other commercial goods, and captives were "purchased" on credit. Indeed, if capital was the catalyst for the transatlantic slave system, credit was the driving force that kept the system in motion. For African societies, the cannibalizing and capitalist impact of transatlantic slaving was enormous and as unquantifiable as the number of Africans removed from their homelands first to Europe and then to the Americas and Asia in the last half millennium.

INTERPRETING TRANSATLANTIC SLAVING THROUGH METAPHORS AND IDIOMS

The problem of interpreting transatlantic slaving from the perspectives of the enslaved is usually decried in several ways. First, very few sources pregnant with such views exist and certainly not for the major slaving regions in Africa or in the Americas. Second, because of this state of affairs, it is a zero-sum game to rely on "European" sources in order to arrive at "African" thoughts and feelings around their bonded experiences. Third, where African idioms and metaphors exist as interpretive devices, these simply boil down to irrational beliefs about

---

[3] George Fitzhugh, *Cannibals All! Or, Slaves Without Masters* (Richmond, Va.: A. Morris, 1857), 27, 175.

[4] Cited in David Eltis and David Richardson, *Atlas of the Transatlantic Slave Trade* (New Haven, Conn.: Yale University Press, 2011), 68; Daniel Defoe, vol. 9, *Defoe's Review*, 89, cited in *Robinson Crusoe*, ed. Evan R. Davis (Peterborough, Ontario, Canada: Broadview Press, 2010), 26.

"witchcraft" or the fear of "cannibalism," and thus are of little value to the historian or whoever writes about transatlantic slaving. Over the past few decades, however, we have come to know much more about African lives under captivity beyond statistics and sources that more or less talk about African (diasporic) views and values. Indeed, the growing number of studies of slaving processes in and outside of Africa—and where African peoples are the subject—make it clear that African narratives of enslavement do in fact provide integral insights about *their* lives with a greater geographical reach than previously thought. Whatever the technical constraints placed on their voices, the available firsthand accounts is not only rich with important perspectives but force us to grapple with them in new ways and to seriously employ their self-understandings and idioms to the task at hand.

Grappling with Ghosts

One of the best ways to interpret the impact of transatlantic slaving is through the lived experiences of generations who successfully left some record or recollection containing important truths that radiated beyond the circumference of the individual. North American "slave narratives" contain one such set of recollections. But these narratives were largely crafted for an audience potentially sympathetic to the abolitionists' cause and where, more importantly, the North American experience of the (formerly) enslaved was paramount. In this way, the abolitionists reasoned, fugitive or formerly enslaved testimonies framing the evils and brutality of enslavement would effectively buttress the fight to end chattel slavery, and therefore few tellers shared and even fewer amanuenses asked about the "African" experience of those willing to provide their account. Viewed from this perspective on narrative construction, it is thus very significant for us to find anywhere from a paragraph to large number of pages devoted to the African experiences of the enslaved and even more crucial to locate in those pages interpretations of the impact of transatlantic slaving for those born *outside* of Africa. The disembodied spirits of captive Africans wander among the living through their preserved narratives but, in unexpected ways, offering nuanced perspectives on the processes of Atlantic slaving that they and their ancestors endured.

In grappling with the stories of these disembodied spirits, invoked when we cite their names or narratives, we began to come to terms with one of the diasporic groups impacted by transatlantic slaving and how they attempted to make sense of its trauma and trepidation. For those born "free," North American enslavement was "that abominable, vampirish, and bloody system," cannibalizing the flesh and soul of the enslaved.[5] Among those with an enslaved experience and with an interpretive voice, all used words and phrases such as "successful robbers," "enslavers," "captured," "suffered in the middle passage," "kidnapped," "horrid," and "their business was to steal negroes from Africa" as proxies for what could not be expressed in written language alone. Almost all used the word "stolen" to refer to their or their ancestors' removal from an African homeland and their eviction from humanity. The leading nineteenth-century abolitionist and orator Frederick Douglass (1818–1895) poignantly summarized a wider understanding of transatlantic slaving: "The more I read, the more I was led to abhor and detest my enslavers. I could regard them in no other light than a band of successful robbers, who had left their homes, and gone to Africa, and stolen us from our homes, and in a strange land reduced us to slavery."[6] The wrongful taking and carrying away of individuals and kin remained thematic for individuals like John Brown, who indicated in his account, "His father had been stolen from Africa. He was of the Eboe tribe," while Samuel Ringgold (1817–1866) viewed transatlantic slaving as a seismic rupture between he and his ancestry, recalling, "My father . . . was descended from an African prince. [This information] comes to me simply from tradition – such tradition as poor slaves may maintain. Like the sources of the Nile, my ancestry, I am free to admit, is rather difficult of tracing."[7] For John Andrew Jackson of South Carolina, his "grandfather was [also] stolen from Africa," but his "father learned the African method of curing snake bites, and was in consequence, called Dr. Clavern," demonstrating that such transference of (therapeutic) knowledge was not a simple function of rote "tradition" but an Africa-based healing institution which, in its continuance, resisted the corrosive effects of transatlantic slaving.[8]

---

[5] Cited in Jon Christian Suggs, *Whispered Consolations: Law and Narrative in African American Life* (Ann Arbor: University of Michigan Press, 2000), 39.

[6] Frederick Douglass, *Narrative of the Life of Frederick Douglass, an American Slave. Written by Himself* (Boston: Anti-Slavery Office, 1845), 40.

[7] John Brown, *Slave Life in Georgia: A Narrative of the Life, Sufferings, and Escape of John Brown, a Fugitive Slave, Now in England* (London: W. M. Watts, 1855), 1–2; Samuel Ringgold, *Autobiography of a Fugitive Negro: His Anti-Slavery Labours in the United States, Canada, & England* (London: John Snow, 1855), 5.

[8] John Andrew Jackson, *The Experience of a Slave in South Carolina* (London: Passmore & Alabaster, 1862), 7.

In Samuel Ringgold's sentiment, however, there is another story: transatlantic slaving made "tracing" memory and one's ancestry improbable for many, and the capstone of this anguish and rupture was the imposition of a new name and thus an enslaved memory. "My ancestors were transported from Africa to America," recalled Mattie Jackson (1846–1910), "at the time the slave trade flourished in the Eastern States. I cannot give dates, as my progenitors, being slaves, had no means of keeping them. By all accounts my great grandfather was captured and brought from Africa. *His original name I never learned.*"[9] For Jacob Stroyer (1849–1908), the same was true for his father, who "was brought from Africa when but a boy and was sold to the Colonel's father, old Col. Dick Singleton. . . . I did not learn what name father went by before he was brought to this country, I only know that he stated that Col. Dick Singleton gave him the name of William, by which name he was known to the day of his death."[10] The imposition of William or the name Mattie's great grandfather assumed signaled—at least in the mind of the slaveholder—a temporal break from both men's African identity and kin and, eventually, a replacement of memory with one authored by the enslaver. Consequently, the "name he was known to the day of his death" became a mnemonic for a fictitious "new" history as William and by which all, including the person so named, would remember him(self). For those who sought out their African past through the literature of their time, they too received grossly fictional accounts designed to reinforce pejorative ideas about Africans and about the diasporic reader of those books. Amanda Smith (1837–1915) tells us, "I remembered when I was quite young I had heard my father and mother talk about Africa. I remembered, too, that I used to see a large paper, away back in the forties, called 'The Brother Jonathan Almanac.' . . . It had large pictures, and Africans in their costumes and huts, and Indians in their wigwams, great boa constrictors, bears, lions and panthers; and some of the pictures were horrid, as I remember

---

[9] Mattie J. Jackson, *The Story of Mattie J. Jackson: Her Parentage, Experience of Eighteen Years in Slavery, Incidents During the War, Her Escape from Slavery* (Lawrence, Mass.: Sentinel Office, 1866), 3 (emphasis added).

[10] Jacob Stroyer, *Sketches of My Life in the South. Part I* (Salem, Mass.: Salem Press, 1879), 9.

them now."[11] Indeed, remembering and the inability to locate memory, and thus ancestry, affected those whom we will never know and those whom we know much about, including the likes of Booker T. Washington (1856–1915), who wrote the following:

> *Of my ancestry I know almost nothing.* While in slave quarters, and even later, I heard whispered conversations among the colored people of the tortures which the slaves, including, no doubt, my ancestors on my mother's side, suffered in the middle passage of the slave ship while being conveyed from Africa to America. *I have been unsuccessful in securing information that would throw any accurate light upon the history of my family beyond my mother.* She, I remember, had a half-brother and a half-sister. In the days of slavery, not very much attention was given to family history and family records – that is, black family records. My mother, I suppose, attracted the attention of a purchaser who was afterward my owner and hers. Her addition to the slave family attracted about as much attention as the purchase of a new horse or cow. Of my father I know even less than of my mother....[12]

If one wants to know how diasporic Africans interpreted transatlantic and domestic forms of enslavement, they need go no further than to imagine the look in Booker T. Washington's eyes as he penned those words or the lives of many lesser known enslaved or formerly enslaved individuals. In the case of Isaac Johnson (1844–1905) of Kentucky, naming and ancestry were intimately shaped by the "villainous vocation of the Slave Trade." "For reasons that will appear before the end is reached," he explains, "my surname is the maiden name of my mother. As I look back to my boyhood days I can see that my mother was an intelligent woman, considering her station in life, and it is from her, and my paternal uncles in after years, I learned as to my ancestry. . . . My grandfather was an Irishman, named Griffin Yeager, and his brothers were engaged in the villainous vocation of the Slave Trade. Their business was to steal Negroes from Africa or wherever they could get them and sell them as slaves in the United States. My mother was stolen by these people from the island of

---

[11] Amanda Smith, *An Autobiography: The Story of the Lord's Dealings with Mrs. Amanda Smith, the Colored Evangelist: Containing an Account of Her Life Work of Faith, and Her Travels in America, England, Ireland, Scotland, India, and Africa as an Independent Missionary* (Chicago: Meyer & Brother Publishers, 1893), 215.

[12] Booker T. Washington, *An Autobiography: The Story of My Life and Work* (Naperville, Ill.: J. L. Nichols & Co., 1901), 32–33 (emphasis added).

Madagascar in the year 1840. She was brought to America and given to my grandfather who concluded she would make a good servant. He gave her the name of Jane and kept her till he died."[13] More than mother's breast milk, enslaved African women provided other vital nutriment in the form of teachings, memory, and connecting progeny with ancestry. "Then mother would talk of Africa," Thomas Lewis Johnson (1836–1921) recalled fondly, "how that they were once all free there, but white people stole us from our country and made slaves of us. This appeared to be all she knew of the matter. . . . My mother's advice and my mother's teaching will ever remain fresh in my memory."[14]

As memory eroded in some, others knew very well how slavery cannibalized memory and kinship and, in turn, responded by remembering and reconstituting bonds against the risk of rupture. While the parents of William H. Robinson (1848–1923) also originated in "Madagascar," Samuel Hall (1818–1912) remembered, "forefathers [who] were full-blooded Africans. My father could well remember when he was shipped over. He was born in Liberia and he and his mother were kidnap[p]ed when he was 15 years of age and they were brought over to this country and sold as slaves. The mother never would work, but pined away and died. She never learned the American language. My father had two brothers who were never brought over."[15] Emma J. Ray's (1859–1930) "great grandfather was [also] brought from Africa," but it was her father who knew the divisive impact of slavery and "was very much troubled at the prospect of seeing his wife, my mother, sold, and became restless, consequently his young master bought us just to please my father, as he threatened to run away."[16] Lastly, for Sam Aleckson (1852–1914), his "great grandfather came . . . from Africa," but he did "not know the name [his] great grandfather bore in Africa, [for] when he arrived in this country he was given the name, Clement, and when he found he needed a surname – something he was not

13 Isaac Johnson, *Slavery Days in Old Kentucky. A True Story of a Father Who Sold His Wife and Four Children. By One of the Children* (Ogdensburg, N.Y.: Republican & Journal Print, 1901), 7–8.
14 Thomas Lewis Johnson, *Twenty-Eight Years a Slave, or the Story of My Life in Three Continents* (Bournemouth, U.K.: W. Mate & Sons, 1909), 4.
15 William H. Robinson, *From Log Cabin to the Pulpit, or, Fifteen Years in Slavery* (Eau Clair, Wisc.: James H. Tifft, 1913), 11; Samuel Hall, *47 Years a Slave: A Brief Story of His Life before and After Freedom Came to Him* (Washington, Iowa: Journal Print, 1912), 26.
16 Emma J. Ray, *Twice Sold, Twice Ransomed: Autobiography of Mr. and Mrs. L. P. Ray* (Chicago: Frees Methodist Publishing House, 1926), 15.

accustomed to in his native land – he borrowed that of the man who bought him."[17] As the above accounts demonstrate, many knew at least their great-grandparents and of the corrosive forces of slavery but worked against such forces by seeking ancestors and by connecting to a memory deeper than the "new" name the enslaved received upon birth or entry into slave society. Those accounts also demonstrate that though the enslaved in North America and the Caribbean rarely referred to whites as cannibals per se, they employed analogous idioms, such as "backra/buckra" and "cracker," to refer to exclusively "white people" whose "crack" of the whip made the "back raw"—that is, an eating away of human flesh through the terror and violence of the iconic whip. Indeed, and in spite of the nebulous linguistic origins of the pan-American term "backra/buckra," its meaning and target was without doubt when either Harriet Tubman of North America used it or when Mary Prince of the Caribbean did the same to talk about the "wickedness" of "the Buckra men."[18]

The Cravings of Cannibals and Capitalists

Having served almost a decade of bondage in Kano and Katsina in present-day northern Nigeria, Ali Eisami Garinambe and unnamed others were sold to "the white men" who "brought us to the sea-shore, brought a very small canoe, and transferred us one by one to the large vessel" in about 1818. "The people of the great vessel," Ali remarked, "were wicked." These "wicked" people were in fact Spaniards, the first and the last breed of transatlantic capitalists, trafficking in a period where British efforts to suppress transatlantic slaving were meager at best and where West Africans such as Ali continued to interpret the cannibalizing effects of slavers in familiar idiom. After three months below deck, a British antislaving vessel intercepted the Spanish slave ship that carried Ali and others. He then became one of almost 180,000 "liberated" Africans resettled in British colonies or places under British jurisdictions after 1807, about half of which, including Ali, were brought to the British colony of Sierra Leone. But if the enslaving

[17] Sam Aleckson, *Before the War, and After the Union: An Autobiography* (Boston: Gold Mind, 1929), 17–18.
[18] Mary Prince, *The History of Mary Prince, a West Indian Slave. Related by Herself...* (London: F. Westley and A. H. Davis, 1831), 13; Sarah H. Bradford, *Harriet, the Moses of Her People* (New York: Geo. R. Lockwood and Son, 1886), 93, 98, 104, 106; Kate Larson, *Bound for the Promised Land: Harriet Tubman: Portrait of an American Hero* (New York: One World Books, 2004), 205.

Spaniards were "wicked," Ali and his co-captives viewed the British "emancipators" as cannibals, In one scene Ali is taken to a house in Freetown and his co-captives immediately thought, "the white man has taken Ali, and put him into the house, in order to slaughter him [for consumption]."[19] Two decades after Ali's departure from his homeland, Kaweli (James Covey) served as interpreter for the Mende-speaking captives onboard the Spanish slaver *La Amistad*, but one of those male captives, named Konoma, was singularly and curiously described as "one who was supposed to be a cannibal." Though this description came from Kaweli and from Yale University professor Josiah Gibbs, who reportedly learned some Mende from Kaweli, it was based more on the racial thinking of the white complier of the account, John Barber, than on Kaweli's translation, since Konoma's language was "not readily understood by Covey, the interpreter."[20]

Unlike the other 35 *Amistad* captives, whose brief biographical sketches were punctuated by details first on family and second on mechanism of enslavement, Barber focused on Konoma's "large lips," "projecting mouth," and his filed "incisor teeth," which, taken together, gave "him rather a savage appearance."[21] No doubt Africans, in bondage or not, understood and at times described other "Africans" as cannibals, but rarely did they do so in the transatlantic era and with the connotation of devouring the person and transforming their bodies into a commodity or iconic transatlantic objects such as red wine, cheese, gunpowder, and flags for ships. In effect, captive Africans interpreted their "African" captors or patrons variously and contradictorily: Ali said little of his Fula, Hausa, and Yorùbá holders or the "Katanga King," in whose house he was kept while in bondage and who told him, "I will not treat him ill." Eventually, his Yorùbá holder ceded him to the "wicked" Spaniards, whose misfortune and inability to bring their captives to a Cuban market brought Ali to Sierra Leone, where Ali thought the British "white man" would "slaughter him" for consumption. Kaweli too was bonded in a ruler's house for some years,

---

[19] Sigismund Wilhelm Koelle, "A Biographical Sketch of Ali Eisami Gazir," in *African Native Literature, or Proverbs, Tales, Fables . . .* , ed. Sigismund Wilhelm Koelle (London: Church Missionary House, 1854), 254–55.

[20] John W. Barber, *A History of the Amistad Captives: Being A Circumstantial Account of the Capture of the Spanish Schooner Amistad, by the Africans on Board; Their Voyage, and Capture near Long Island, New York; with Biographical Sketches of Each of the Surviving Africans . . .* (New Haven, Conn.: E. L. & J. W. Barber, 1840), 15.

[21] Ibid., 10.

after being seized by three men from his parents' house and before a
thwarted Atlantic voyage on a Portuguese slave ship. He tells us the
ruler's wife for whom he planted rice "treated him with great kindness." Samuel Crowther, a Yorùbá, was also ceded to the Portuguese—
whose encounter with Crowther "was not without great fear and
trembling"—in addition to viewing the British who rescued him as
"new conquerors, whom we at first very much dreaded."[22] Kaweli, Ali,
and Samuel eventually found themselves in Sierra Leone as "liberated"
Africans on account of British naval intervention. After their rescue
and baptisms, all shifted their views of the (British) "white man" as
cannibalizing capitalists to Christianizing champions against the
very Atlantic slavery which the British dominated.[23]

But those views, and the cannibalistic and capitalistic impulses
that shaped them, were often mediated by a Christian calling *after*
successful proselyzation, especially in Christianizing and European
(colonial) enclaves in Africa and the Americas. With or without a
Christian filter, enslaved and baptized Africans, such as José Monzolo
of Kôngo, Ignacio de Angola, and Francisco Yolofo de Guinea, all "believed that [those] whom they called whites brought them to kill them
and to make the flags for the ships from their remains." Jesuit priest
Alonso De Sandoval, who worked in Cartagena where the foregoing
individuals were found, noted during the Atlantic crossing that the
enslaved from the Guinea coast and Angola became "very sad and
melancholy, believing they will be rendered into fat and eaten."[24] In
the 1760s, Christian G. A. Oldendorp, a Moravian clergyman, interviewed "baptized slaves" from west and west-central Africa domiciled
in the Danish Caribbean colonies. In one interview with a "Congo
Black," Oldendorp recorded that this unnamed individual "made a
large journey in his country and was abducted during it by *body
snatchers* and sold to a Danish ship. Another one had the same fate

---

[22] Samuel Crowther, "Letter of Mr. Samuel Crowther to the Rev. William Jowett, in
1837, then secretary of the Church Missionary Society, detailing the circumstances
connected with his being sold as a slave," in James Frederick Schon and Samuel
Crowther, *Journals of the Rev. James Frederick Schon and Mr. Samuel Crowther
who, with the Sanction of Her Majesty's Government, Accompanied the Expedition
up the Niger in 1841 in Behalf of the Church Missionary Society* (London: Hatchard
and Son, 1842), 380–81.

[23] Koelle, "Biographical Sketch," 253; Barber, *Amistad Captives*, 15.

[24] Alonso De Sandoval, *Treatise on Slavery: Selections from De Instauranda Aeth-
iopum Salute*, ed. and trans. Nicole von Germeten (Indianapolis, Ind.: Hackett
Publishing, 2008), 56.

through treachery. Some of his countrymen had arranged with the *body snatchers*, who lived far away from him, that they should take him if they brought him to a certain place. It did happen. He was brought to a packing facility where certain Blacks have always slaves ready to supply the Europeans and from there he came on a European ship."[25] These "body snatchers" represented at once the deep penetration of Atlantic capital (or credit) and its cannibalism into communities hundreds of miles removed from the Atlantic coast and signaled, as one key indicator, how enslaved Africans viewed the impact of Atlantic enslavement on their political and social lives. Oldendorp also interviewed several captives originating from a wide area between Loango and Ndongo (Angola), where all specified how members of their own communities and, at times, their own families snatched them away—one man's mother "had sold his brother," and another man was ceded "to Blacks of his own nation, who traded him, further to the Loango and these traded him to an English slave ship." In other related instances, a "black woman of this nation was, while she was going somewhere, captured by her countrymen, sold to the Loango and brought by those to a Dutch ship," while another "Mandongo Black was also made a slave by his own countrymen, who invaded his region. They chased him until the evening when they caught him and sold him afterwards." This inward feasting on one's "countrymen" is indeed metaphorical, but, in at least one instance, enslaved Africans who refused to eat on board a slave vessel to Barbados were literally forced to eat each other: an English ship caption "ordered his crew to lay hands on the most obstinate of them and to hack that poor creature into small pieces. Thereupon he forced several of the others to eat a piece of the mutilated body and thereby assured and promised them that he would the remaining ones, one after the other, torture like that, if they would not consent to eat. This horrifying deed had the desired effect that the Blacks began to eat again."[26] Though forced cannibalism targeting the flesh and the psychology of the enslaved was one form of transatlantic consumption, the near-universal belief in European/white cannibalism was much more pervasive and, indeed,

---

[25] Christian George Andreas Oldendorp, *Historie der caribischen Inseln Sanct Thomas, Sanct Crux und Sanct Jan, insbesondere der dasigen Neger und der Mission der evangelischen Brüder-Unität Herrnhut, Erster Teil*, eds. Gudrun Meier et al. (Berlin: Staatliches Museum für Völkerkunde Dresden, 2000), I: 488 (emphasis added).
[26] Ibid., I: 488, 508.

trans-Atlantic—that is, beyond the Atlantic Ocean. Interpretations of enslavement as cannibalism and Christian conversion as rescue from it connected Atlantic and Indian Ocean slaving—at the level of African perspectives and of slaving as a process—in nineteenth-century central and southeast Africa.

Atlantic capital and slaving extended into or merged with the currents of Indian Ocean slaving before the mid-eighteenth century when Madagascar became the primary source of most southeast African captives exported to the Americas. After the mid-eighteenth century, the greater part of these captives were drawn from mainland southeast Africa—and especially among Makua, Yao, and Bisa peoples—but in spite of the distance and the high death tolls between this mainland and the Atlantic, southeast Africa, including the Portuguese colony of Mozambique, became a major supplier of captives to the Americas during the late eighteenth and nineteenth centuries. With human exports growing at a rapid pace and with French, Dutch, and Portuguese commercial forces in competition for captives, British efforts to suppress international enslavement in the nineteenth century also extended to east central and southeast Africa, where the trafficking in the enslaved to Indian, Arabian, and local or regional markets, such as the Dutch Cape province, continued unabated. But the British attempt to suppress international slaving north of the equator after 1815 was constrained by a number of factors, not least of which was the Mozambique port of Quelimane becoming a major embarkation point after 1815, and where Brazil, particularly Rio de Janeiro, dominated the south Atlantic traffic. For those not destined for the Atlantic, their experiences and perspectives sharply parallel those captives who made the Atlantic crossing.

In the nineteenth century, Chilekwa, Rashid bin Hassani, and Chisi Ndjurisiye Sichyajunga were all Bisa or, in Chisi's words, of "the Biza [Bisa] country." Captured by strangers at the age of 10, Chilekwa was taken to the east African coast and back, only to find his mother, who, unfortunately, failed to ransom him, making her "very sad and [she] cried bitterly and I cried bitterly too, 'Woe is me, mother,' because I was leaving my mother and my relations and my country." While on an Arab slaving dhow (sailing/trading vessel) bound for Oman, British antislaving vessels seized the dhow and landed the captives as freed individuals at Muscat. During the seizure, Chilekwa recalled, "A European and a black man peered down into the lower deck and . . . when we saw the face of the European we were terrified. We were quite certain that Europeans eat people. . . . [After the rescue] some of us thought that the Europeans were tricking us and that they meant to fatten us, so that they might eat us and make our bones into sweetmeats. And we thought that the brown sugar which they gave us was made out of the bones of our fellows who had been captured before us." Eventually, "We forgot all our fears," Chilekwa tells us, "when we were slaves and expecting to be killed and eaten and to have our bones made into sugar by the Europeans, but we felt sad about being far from our relations and our homes and we wondered what our end would be."[27] But in the end, and as the stories of Ali Garinambe and Samuel Crowther showed, Chilekwa not only worked for the British antislaving campaign onboard the *Osprey*, but, as a converted Christian, he now saw his captive experiences as his path to salvation: "There have been many ups and downs in my lifetime, but I thank my Lord Jesus for all He has done for me, by saving me from the power of death and by helping me to serve Him in His missionary work."[28] Kibuli bin Mchubiri (renamed Rashid bin Hassani) was captured at the age of 12 in a raid on his village after his sister was brutally killed. After Kibuli was sold several times, he landed in Zanzibar, where he "was terrified and thought, 'Here I shall be killed and eaten.' Out came an enormously fat woman with gold ear-rings and gold nose-rings. I thought, 'She is as fat as that from eating men.'"[29] Eventually, Kibuli would become a Muslim, marry, and obtain his freedom; though his account lacks the missionary zeal of Chilekwa's, both individuals speak to the transoceanic interpretation of international slaving as cannibalism.

The cannibalism of captivity and the loss of (male) kin protectors operated literally but quite differently for Chisi and for her Yao contemporary Swema. After Chisi's mother was killed from wounds inflicted by a lion, she was seized by warriors who executed all the men and took the women, including her, as their captive wives. Swema's father was also killed by a lion, followed by a locust invasion destroying the crops, famine, and a disease epidemic. Death cuts Swema off from her older sisters and her infant brother, while the husband of Chisi cuts off her ear. Chisi immediately began to scream and call out, "Woe

---

[27] Petro Kilekwa, *Slave Boy to Priest: The Autobiography of Padre Petro Kilekwa*, trans. K. H. Nixon Smith (London: Universities' Mission to Central Africa, 1937), 10, 15. See also C. W. B. Arnold, "Slave-Boy to Priest," *The Nyasaland Journal* 2, no. 1 (Jan. 1949): 7–15.

[28] Ibid., 63.

[29] Margery Perham, ed., *Ten Africans* (London: Faber and Faber, 1936), 93, 98 (quote), 99.

FIGURE 4 Group of Enslaved Africans in Zanzibar, ca. 1883. (English School, (19th century) / Private Collection / © Michael Graham-Stewart / The Bridgeman Art Library.)

is me that I have no relations," which her husband, Ndeye, confirmed by exclaiming, "It is true that if this woman had relations I should have to atone for the ear I have struck off." Swema's mother was torn from her daughter and in the forced separation is left to die un- mourned outside of her homeland. Swema fought the separation from her mother while being beaten with sticks but no longer had the will to live and had to be carried and force-fed, though one of the captor's assistants asked, "Why should we carry this cadaver any longer? You can easily see that this little girl is only good for the vultures to eat." Swema then journeys on a dhow to Zanzibar, and the voyage is com- parable to the experiences of other Africans on the Atlantic circuit. Because Swema is unable to rise upon their arrival, the captors—the Arab caravan leader and his superior—view her as a "cadaver" to be buried at a cemetery, and she is indeed buried alive in a shallow grave. Miraculously, Swema is rescued by a young man from the Indian Ocean island of Réunion who heard her sobbing and brought her to the French Spiritains' mission in Zanzibar Town. The rest of Swema's narrative relates her struggles with accepting Christianity, especially when she is ordered by the Sister in charge at the mission clinic to treat the wounds of the very Arab leader of her slave caravan! For Chisi, she too would find herself at a (German Moravian) mission sta- tion in Utengule, where "All I understood was the name, Jesus Christ from above," after which she is baptized following five years of almost futile study with the mission.[30] Swema was baptized as Madeleine but was renamed Marie Antoinette ten years after relating her account.[31] For Swema, Chisi, Kibuli, and Chilekwa, the unfolding episodes of capture, captivity, and cannibalism were points in the same enslavement process that drew individuals away from "home" and loved ones—the cruelty of kinlessness. Above all, the multileveled craving for flesh (labor) and the capital generated for and by it included a postabolition appetite for Christian and Muslim converts who would be encouraged to create new communities among fellow strangers rather than return "home" to known kinfolks.

INTERPRETING ABOLITIONISM THROUGH METAPHORS AND IDIOMS

In the age of abolition, where most slave-trafficking European nations slowly and grudgingly conceded to the antislaving campaign led by Britain's "moral capital" and naval forces along the western African littoral, international enslavement increased dramatically on the eastern African coast, often extending its reach deep into the east central and southeast African hinterlands.[32] In effect, and at a time when antislaving efforts and shifting European/white sentiments toward enslavement in overseas colonies matured into a legislative abolitionist

[30] Marcia Wright, *Strategies of Slaves & Women: Life-Stories from East/Central Africa* (New York and London: Lilian Barber Press and James Currey, 1993), 81, 89–90. See also Elise Kootz-Kretschmer, *Sichyajunga, ein Leben in Unruhe* (Herrnhut, Gremany: Missions-Buchhandlung, 1938); idem, *Stories of Old Times*, trans. M. Bryan (London: Sheldon Press, 1932).

[31] Swema's account, under the name Madeleine, can be found in the Archives générales de la Congrégation du Saint-Esprit, 2K1.1b5., file no. 108668, in "Histoire de Magdeleine racontée par elle-même aux petites filles de la mission de Zanzibar" (dated March 12, 1869) and "Histoire d'une petite esclave enterrée vivante ou l'Amour filial," a 32-page manuscript containing P. Horner's unpaginated French translation of Swema's original Ki-Swahili account. For a copy of this French translation and the context of the document, see Edward A. Alpers, "The Story of Swema: Female Vulnerability in Nineteenth-Century East Africa," in Claire C. Robertson and Martin A. Klein, eds., *Women and Slavery in Africa* (Madison: The University of Wisconsin Press, 1983), 185–219.

[32] On the anti-slaving and abolitionist movements in Britain, see Christopher Leslie Brown, *Moral Capital: Foundations of British Abolitionism* (Chapel Hill: University of North Carolina Press, 2006); Seymour I. Drescher, *Capitalism and Antislavery: British Popular Mobilization in Comparative Perspective* (New York: Oxford University Press, 1987).

movement, the center of international slavery also shifted from west and west-central Africa to the periphery of Atlantic slaving in east central and southeast Africa. At the level of process, there was little difference between Atlantic and Indian Ocean slaveries since both were underwritten by non-African trade goods and capital, and thus does it really matter if Cape Town, as a metaphor for the link or distance between these two oceanic zones, belongs to the Indian Ocean or Atlantic world? Indeed, in both zones and in variants in between, plantation-based slavery was but one form of coerced labor and reculturalization (e.g., renaming, reclothing, and remaking humans into chattel). Accompanied by mass insecurities, due to intense human and uncontrollable natural forces, much of the same thematic experiences of the Atlantic continued and some of the same interpretive lenses were used by locally based and exported eastern African captives to make sense of their lives. These "liberated" Africans were often denied the right or means to return to mainland Africa and instead served lengthy indentures in places like Mombasa, Zanzibar, Muscat, Bombay, Aden, the Seychelles, Durban, and Mauritius. Close to an estimated 1 million people from eastern Africa were exported to Asia, especially Arabia, in the nineteenth century. Corrupt officials, seamen, and translators associated with British antislaving efforts in the western Indian Ocean facilitated such exportations by condemning legitimate vessels and enslaving free African individuals, especially in the second half of the nineteenth century. Free-turned-captive and "liberated" Africans were usually assigned gendered laboring roles: women and children were placed with Christian missions and used for domestic service, while men did manual labor in harbors, railways, and on plantations. Domiciled in these sites, African metaphors and idioms of captivity, as well as longings for home and family, were critical tools found in their accounts and often used to grasp the meaning of their life stories.

The Center in the Periphery

As studies of slaveries have moved from the margin to the center of "modern historical scholarship," in James Walvin's view, so too must eastern Africa and the western Indian Ocean move from a peripheral phenomenon to the center of histories that connect with the Atlantic, especially in the nineteenth century.[33] In that century, the absence of

---

[33] James Walvin, *Questioning Slavery* (New York: Routledge, 1995), vii.

FIGURE 5   Liberated Africans on Deck of the *Wildfire*, ca. 1860. After leaving New York for the Congo River and then Cuba, the slave ship *Wildfire* was intercepted by U.S. anti-slaving vessels, and the vessel and her captives were eventually brought to Liberia. (Harper's Weekly (June 2, 1860), vol. 4, p.344 / Library of Congress.)

male or state protection exacerbated female and child vulnerabilities, as the cases of Chisi and Swema show, and thus made many more likely to be captured or, ironically, to voluntarily seek out captivity in return for stable meals, protection in a predatory environment, and the opportunity to belong among cultural members or strangers. For Narwimba, abolition and antislaving efforts held little if any reverence. Her circumstances, shaped by the "terror" of "ferocious enemies" and the death of her first husband and 9 out of 12 children, led to her capture and a bold escape made possible by renaming herself (Namira) and then sneaking away at night, eventually reaching her natal village, where all were "very happy, they greeted and embraced me, and after I had told them everything that had happened to me, they shouted . . . [p]raise and thanks that [I] have escaped from the enemy."[34] No abolitionist or anti-slaving squadron came to her rescue; the engineering of her escape and reconnection with kin—and again after leaving a Christian mission to be with her son and grandchildren—was all her own. Such African initiatives, including kin redemption, were part of an arsenal of strategic responses to increased domestic and regional forms of bondage and against the cannibalism of kinlessness.[35] In fact, after a few years at the Moravian mission station, the missionary who recorded Narwimba's story "tried to comfort her, but she [Narwimba] looked past me, shook her head and said: 'I can't endure it any longer, I must go to my son. Now you say, here there is peace and no more disputes around me and my granddaughter as there was earlier. But when you come to my house one day, and find it empty, you will know where I have gone.'" The missionaries "would have kept the friendly old woman at the station with us and would have discouraged against traveling; but now the longing [had] become too powerful within her. She went to her son and there she hugged her grandchildren and rejoiced over them."[36]

Kinless victims of nineteenth-century slaving in east Africa, approximately 100 African boys between the ages 9 and 21 were retrieved from Arab slave ships by British antislaving squadrons and interviewed over a 5-year period at the Universities' Mission headquartered in Zanzibar. The mission was "formed by Church of England enthusiasts in response to David Livingston's call to action after his return to England from the Zambezi expedition."[37] The texts of the interviews were written in Ki-Swahili and translated by an editor, who laid out the narrative structure of their stories this way: "Nearly

---

[34] Elise Kootz-Kretschmer, *Großmutter Narwimba: Was sie erlebte und was sie erlitt* (Herrnhut, Germany: Missions-Buchhandlung [Basler Mission], 1925), 5–9.
[35] For other African initiatives on the theme of abolition, especially on the Gold Coast, see Kwabena O. Akurang-Parry, "We Shall Rejoice to See the Day When Slavery Shall Cease to Exist": The Gold Coast Times, the African Intelligentsia, and Abolition in the Gold Coast, *History in Africa* 31 (2004): 19–42.
[36] Kootz-Kretschmer, *Großmutter Narwimba*, 23.
[37] Edward A. Alpers, "Representations of Children in the East African Slave Trade," *Slavery and Abolition* 30, no. 1 (2009): 33.

all the boys write (1) first of their homes, (2) then of their separation from home and sure gravitation into the hands of Arab slave-dealers, (3) the march of the slave-caravan from the interior to the coast, (4) the disposal of the slaves, either on the coast or by exportation, [and] (5) finally, their transfer to British hands and consignment to the Universities' Mission." Having digested these stories, the editor concluded, "War and famine are the ruling factors in African life, and the Slave-trade is the sure support when not the prime cause of both." In other words, slaving was the common denominator in the frequent bouts of war and famine on land, and at sea the dhow was "a den of horrors, without space to move, or food beyond uncooked grain or fruit, without water for days altogether, while a child's wailing is sufficient reason for throwing it to the sharks." Like their European counterparts, Arab captors were also well aware of the belief in slaving as cannibalism and would duly inform their African captives that "one worse fate that could befall them is to be captured by the white man, whose only object is to fatten and eat them," in an otherwise "speedy consumption by the white-faced cannibals."[38] One "Nyasa boy" was captured and removed from his natal village, but his captor "was himself only a slave," originally "a prisoner taken in war." Among his Yao captors, he "learnt the Yao language" but "forgot my own." He was then sold to "the Arabs in exchange for a woman," eventually landing in Kilwa, where "the Arab of Kilwa sold me to an Arab of Muscat." British naval forces would intercept the dhow on which he and others were stowed, and below deck he and they were "very much afraid, and said: 'To-day we shall certainly be eaten.'" A British ship would take them to Zanzibar, where he and 10 other boys were baptized.[39] The jagged ebb and flow of this unnamed Nyasa boy's story was, characteristically, typical.

Another captured Nyasa boy "put on board a dhow to go to Pemba," which was intercepted by a British vessel, tells us, "when we were brought biscuit we were afraid to eat it, for we thought it was made of men's bones and given to us to fatten us up, till we were fit to be eaten – when we were all fattened up." A Makua boy was "caught and carried off" to the sea where British naval intervention rescued him and others, but where one of the British sailors "made fun of us and said, 'These [biscuits] are made of people's bones,' and some left

---

[38] A. C. Madan, trans. and ed., *Kiungani: Or Story and History from Central Africa* (London: George Bell and Sons, 1887), 5–6, 9–10.

[39] Madan, *Kiungani*, 23–25, 28–29.

off eating. But another sailor came up and said, 'The man is only making fun of you.' 'It's true,' said the first man, 'don't you listen to him. They have given you these bones of your black brethren on purpose to get you to eat them. Come, eat them up.'" This dialogue offers a rare glimpse into the ways in which captives and captors (or rescuers) deployed the idiom of cannibalism and suggests this metaphor casted a much wider geographical and chronological net over processes of international, regional, and local slaveries. But whether or not these young boys believed they would be devoured was not their primary concern, at least according to their edited accounts. Home and family were the axes around which their consciousness turned. A Bemba boy was delighted when British vessels captured his captor's dhow, "But when I thought about my home, I cried." A Bisa boy did not recall "how I came to leave my mother and father," but he ran away from his captors and "began to go homewards." Unfortunately, he was "kidnapped by some other Arabs," before "Europeans took us away, and put us all in boats" bound for Zanzibar. A Makua boy remembered, "At my home where I was born, I belonged to a family of twelve, and there I lived with them a long time," but his seizure (on account of debt) at a young age and his desire for belonging made him view his Arab captor "like a father" and led him to conclude, "I did not know I was really in slavery." Unlike the Bemba boy, he and others en route to Zanzibar were not joyful with British intervention because "some people said to us, 'You are all going to be eaten.'"[40] As the talk of cannibalism and the fact of kinlessness continued, some young men taken from the "slave depots" off the eastern African coast and "liberated" by the local British Consul's court were simply given "a few shillings for their immediate necessities, or transport to British soil to become so-called free labourers, bound to a term of service on a white man's estate."[41] In fact, "liberated" Africans at the missions in Zanzibar were known as "slaves of the English," as the lives of the enslaved mirrored those of the manumitted in terms of labor and their characteristic renaming and reclothing. "Liberated" Africans in the Americas would have indeed found these characterizations apt and as perhaps the foremost image of abolitionism sketched in their minds and in their endless laboring lives.

---

[40] Ibid., 31–32, 35, 38–40, 44.
[41] Ibid., 11.

The End of the Endless Voyage
of Cannibal and Capitalism?

Abolition of transatlantic slaving and slavery by the British parliament in the first decades of the nineteenth century occurred when both practices were indeed profitable, rather than simply free market capitalism rendering them unprofitable, and this economic reality suggests that economic analysis (such as that by Eric Williams in his 1944 classic, *Capitalism and Slavery*) may not entirely account for the social and ideological movements such as those that terminated the "slave trade" in Britain. This is the position advanced by Seymour Drescher in *Econocide*, originally published in 1977, and by James Walvin in his recent book.[42] Christopher Leslie Brown's recent study, *Moral Capital: Foundations of British Abolitionism*, subscribes to this socio-ideological view. Though there is a case to be made for such a view, the economic argument advanced by Williams and later enlarged by Joseph Inikori, Kenneth Morgan, and recently Nuala Zahedieh still occupies an important place in any analysis of British abolition of international slaving.[43] First, as Nicholas Draper has shown, there was a broader base of social involvement than just the iconic British (absentee) planter in the British Caribbean; slave-owning in Britain was widespread scaled to the size of the capital invested, and this was so early on when "the Royal Society was part of the social and economic order which chose slavery as the most viable means of generating wealth" and as fellows were involved in the administration of the slave colony of Jamaica.[44] Second, British abolition of Atlantic slaving resulted in significant benefits to plantation economies in Cuba and Brazil—through Spanish and Portuguese slavers who continued the trafficking—and therefore extended rather than suffocated the life of Atlantic, and western Indian Ocean, slaving into the late

---

[42] See Seymour Drescher, *Econocide: British Slavery in the Era of Abolition* (Chapel Hill: University of North Carolina Press, 2010); Walvin, *Questioning Slavery*, 158–65.

[43] Joseph E. Inikori, *Africans and the Industrial Revolution in England: A Study in International Trade and Economic Development* (New York: Cambridge University Press, 2002), 148–49, 212, 407–42; Kenneth Morgan, *Slavery, Atlantic Trade and the British Economy, 1660–1800* (New York: Cambridge University Press, 2000); Nuala Zahedieh, *The Capital and the Colonies: London and the Atlantic Economy, 1660–1700* (New York: Cambridge University Press, 2010), 287.

[44] Nicholas Draper, *The Price of Emancipation: Slave-Ownership, Compensation and British Society at the End of Slavery* (New York: Cambridge University Press, 2010), 167; Mark Govier, "The Royal Society, Slavery and the Island of Jamaica, 1660–1700," *Notes and Records of the Royal Society* 53, no. 2 (1999): 203.

nineteenth century. In fact, at least 3 million captive Africans left Africa *after* Britain and the United States ratified acts abolishing international, but not domestic, slavery in 1807–08. Finally, we should note that the financial costs associated with African rebellions on board slave ships and in the overseas colonies played a significant part in the calculus of abolition, in that revolts necessitated additional crew and guns on and insurance for slaving voyages and helped to move slaving vessels further south (of the equator) to west-central Africa where largely Portuguese slavers believed the people to be less rebellious.[45] The Portuguese and Brazil would claim the lion's share of international slaving in the postabolition era, and in addition to the economic argument, which drove these slavers to persevere in the face of calls to terminate, the Africans' experiences of abolition provides a human argument that slaving voyages remained almost endless and where capitalism and Christianity triumphed over moral capital. Such triumph morphed into a fervent Christianizing and commercial mission, otherwise known as "legitimate trade," through converted Africans, who often made or facilitated trade concessions.[46]

By the available "slave trade" statistics, Britain and Portugal/Brazil were the leading nations in international and overseas colonial slaving. It is then not surprising that the nineteenth century witnessed the pivot of Britain toward ending international slaving in order to control the seas so that its industrial commerce could flourish in colonial markets and the resistance of the Portuguese in Portugal and in Brazil to this new order through accelerated human trafficking from Africa to its biggest market in Brazil.[47] Against this backdrop, the experiences

---

[45] On the variable of African agency in terminating Atlantic slaving, see Stephen D. Behrendt, David Eltis, and David Richardson, "The Costs of Coercion: African Agency in the Pre-Modern Atlantic World," *The Economic History Review* 54, no. 3 (2001): 454–76.

[46] The phrase "legitimate trade," coined by abolitionists, supposedly signaled the "transition" from the export of enslaved Africans to the export of produce originating from commercial plantations in Africa, often worked by locally captive peoples (or those who would have been sent to the Americas). It was the idea of bringing the American plantation to the source of labor rather than bringing the African laborers to the overseas plantations. It is often overlooked that after Britain abolished transatlantic slaving, they and other Europeans, including some Africans, used enslaved labor in the production and transport of agricultural exports (cash crops) through plantations established on African soil.

[47] See, for instance, Joseph C. Miller, *Way of Death: Merchant Capitalism and the Angolan Slave Trade, 1730–1830* (Madison: University of Wisconsin Press, 1988); Roquinaldo Ferreira, "The Suppression of the Slave Trade and Slave Departures from Angola, 1830s–1860s," *História Unisinos* 15, no. 1 (April 2011): 2–13.

and thus perspectives of the enslaved—situated between the British and Portuguese spheres of interest—are quite revealing in that they help to move the matter of abolition beyond an economic or ideological movement among Europeans/whites. Born in Ajuda (Ouidah) but living in Bahia (Brazil) for about 14 years, an enslaved man who was baptized and given the Christian name Gorge claimed to have belonged to "the King of Portugal and the Portuguese Nation," and when asked again by judges at the Mixed Commission in Rio de Janeiro if he had another king or nation, he replied, "Yes, Senhor, in Ajuda before having been sold to the whites."[48] Gorge was then asked the same question, but after he was among the whites; he responded, "I was a prisoner in Sierra Leone over ten months, and then was under the power of the King of England." The suffering he experienced in Bahia and that he saw Free-town (Sierra Leone) as a prison led historian Walter Hawthorne to sug-gest that Gorge "viewed 'freedom' as an apprentice [in Sierra Leone] as a state worse than slavery as a[n enslaved] seaman," who was captured by British antislaving squadrons while aboard a Portuguese slaving vessel at the port of Lagos.[49] Though we will never know how Gorge viewed something he did not possess—freedom—his claim to be under one "king" over another and thus one situation rather than another was likely shaped by two critical factors: that, after an Atlantic crossing and 14 years in Brazilian captivity, he had crafted important kinship bonds, and that his rupture from those bonds via a British "capture" (rather than "freedom") and placement among linguistic and cultural strangers in the British "prison" of Sierra Leone was interpreted as incarceration

---

[48] Courts of Mixed Commission were established through treaties between Britain and other European slaving nations, allowing British officials the right to interrogate and condemn suspected slaving vessels. On the operation of these courts, see J. P. Marques, *The Sounds of Silence: Nineteenth-Century Portugal and the Abolition of the Slave Trade* (New York: Berghahn Books, 2006), 46–48, 69–71; R. M. Adderley, "'A Most Useful and Valuable People?' Cultural, Moral and Practical Dilemmas in the Use of Liberated African Labor in the Nineteenth Century Caribbean," in S. R. Frey and B. Wood, eds., *From Slavery to Emancipation in the Atlantic World* (London: Frank Cass, 1999), 60; D. Eltis, *Economic Growth and the Ending of the Transatlantic Slave Trade* (New York: Oxford University Press, 1987), 41, 65, 83–90, 117–18, 126, 142, 150, 180, 198–99; L. Bethell, *The Abolition of the Brazilian Slave Trade: Britain, Brazil and the Slave Trade Question, 1807-1869* (New York: Cambridge University Press, 1970); idem, "The Mixed Commissions for the Suppression of the Transatlantic Slave Trade in the Nineteenth Century," *Journal of African History* 7 (1966): 79–93.

[49] Walter Hawthorne, "Gorge: An African Seaman and his Flights from 'Freedom' back to 'Slavery' in the Early Nineteenth Century," *Slavery and Abolition* 31, no. 3 (Sept. 2010): 411–13, 419.

and not liberation. Recall that, in Gorge's testimony, he had been the subject or prisoner of both African and European sovereigns, but his testimony said nothing about his possession or interpretation of "freedom" because, at the time of interrogation, he was still the "slave" of one Joaquim Carneiro de Campos in Bahia, rented out to the owner of the Portuguese slaver, *Emília*, on which he was seized at Lagos.[50] Thus, his testimony was a narrative of enslavement and an indictment of British abolitionism, revealing, on the one hand, that human bonds and belonging meant more than legislative "freedoms" to the enslaved and, on the other, that British antislaving efforts and British-driven abolitionism fell short of African experiences of its purported liberation. Gorge had carved out the only possible path he could, given the literal and metaphorical trappings of both British induced "freedom" and Brazilian "slavery," by remaining a mobile, leased, and enslaved mariner who, ironically, worked with the fear of European duplicity or African revenge on seemingly endless voyages.[51]

Half of those liberated by British antislaving squadrons in the Atlantic remained in the British Caribbean; most of the rest were settled in Sierra Leone, the center of British antislaving activity, rather than returned to their homelands. However, the opportunity to return many to their homelands was available for those crossing both the Atlantic and the western Indian Ocean. To be sure, nineteenth-century slaving conditions parallel to the Atlantic existed in the western Indian Ocean, and the case of "liberated" Africans is representative in a number of ways for the latter region. Mauritius, a British sugar colony, emancipated the last of its apprentices in 1839—and 1833-34 in the British Caribbean—but "liberated" Africans arriving in the colony decades after were immediately placed under a European (planter) as an apprentice or indentured laborer. Not only were their indentureships often extended well beyond their initial allotment of up to 14 years, but those who wished to return to a known homeland, unlike Indian immigrants in Indian and Atlantic Ocean worlds, were refused the right to do so by colonial officials. Colonial officials at the court of the various mixed commissions—charged with adjudicating cases of illegal international slaving—interviewed captive Africans and recorded their names, ages, height, sex, and, for the purpose of return, birthplaces or

---

[50] On the *Emília*., see Walter Hawthorne, "'Being Now, As It Were, One Family': Shipmate Bonding on the Slave Vessel *Emilia*, in Rio de Janeiro and throughout the Atlantic World," *Luso-Brazilian Review* 45, no. 1 (2008): 53–77.

[51] W. Jeffrey Bolster, *Black Jacks: African American Seamen in the Age of Sail* (Cambridge, Mass.: Harvard University Press, 1998), 52.

homelands. But only in very rare cases did return of the "liberated" African occur. Instead, the vast majority were resettled in places far beyond their homelands, and many also died in transit at the "slave" depots, while others were hospitalized, blinded, deeply depressed with nostalgia of home, and succumbed to mass baptisms and proselytizing during their "liberated" experience. Once in their new country of assignment, many were conscripted into the military service, apprenticed to neo-European governments, indentured as laborers, transshipped throughout the Americas, and coerced into "free" labor contracts in places like Cuba and Brazil without the opportunity to leave.[52] In many ways, the story of Ngeve (renamed Catherine Mulgrave) is instructive, not only because it humanizes these processes for many but also because it shows how the variables of coincidence and Christianity shaped stories like hers, making them known to us. Arguably, without these variables at work and in the unpredictable way they operated, narratives like Ngeve's would been muted under what João Pedro Marques calls the "sounds of silence" in Portuguese slaving and the abolitionism of the nineteenth century.[53]

There have been various explorations into the early life of Ngeve, and these forays have included questions about her origins and African life. Paul Lovejoy was previously convinced that "various accounts state that Catherine [Ngeve] came from Luanda, but her description of her home clearly refers to Cape Town, not Luanda." He later regarded this as a "premature suggestion" and aligned himself with the prevailing chorus in favor of Luanda, Angola. Lovejoy thinks Ngeve was born in about 1820, Ulrike Sill thinks (taking Ngeve's second husband's lead) 1827, and Maureen Warner-Lewis hypothesizes "that she was born around 1822, abducted at about eleven, and became a teacher in Jamaica by 1836." Ngeve's tombstone reads that she was born

---

[52] On these matters, see Rosanne Adderley, *"New Negroes from Africa": Slave Trade Abolition and Free African Settlements in the Nineteenth-Century Caribbean* (Bloomington: Indiana University Press, 2006); Robert Conrad, "Neither Slave nor Free: The Emancipados of Brazil, 1818–1868," *The Hispanic American Historical Review* 53, no. 1 (1973): 50–70; Leslie Bethell, "The Mixed Commissions for the Suppression of the Transatlantic Slave Trade in the Nineteenth Century," *Journal of African History* 7, no. 1 (1966): 70–93. The idea of "neo-European states," and the government officials who manage and represent them, refers to those former oversea colonies/states in the Americas established – through conquest and colonization – by European nationals who built these states on the laws, institutions, languages, and religious and racial ideologies, albeit imperfectly and not without contestation, of their respective European homelands.

[53] João Pedro Marques, *The Sounds of Silence: Nineteenth-Century Portugal and the Abolition of the Slave Trade* (Oxford, U.K.: Berghahn Books, 2006).

on November 19, 1826.[54] Born between 1820 and 1827, Ngeve and her sisters were probably baptized, since her "mulatto" mother, Sofia, was baptized and her relatives had Christian names. Ngeve claimed her mother was from a prominent family and her father was "the son of a chieftain employed in the trading post of a [Portuguese] merchant." Ngeve "describes her home town as a city on the ocean . . . with a large church, a school, two forts. . . . The ships are able to voyage up to the city, there are no breakers. . . . The town itself had a governor, a bishop, monks in various habits, chasubles, choirboys, [and with] holy water."[55] Ngeve's name, meaning "hippopotamus" in Kimbundu and usually given to the second-born twin, links her to the Mbundu or Ovimbundu, who hailed from Angola's southwestern highlands and were famed as hunters, raiders, carriers, and long-distance traders in ivory, captives, and beeswax from the hinterland. It is highly probable, therefore, that one of the two sisters seized along with Ngeve was her older twin, likely named Jamba (from *onjamba*, "elephant"), a name given to the first-born twin. The seizure of individuals or those belonging to well-established families as in the case of Ngeve and her kin was not exceptional, and the capture of Ndombe women like Nbena, who had sufficient socio-political standing in her community in Angola, support this contention. The abolition of slavery in the Portuguese empire came only in 1875–76 and its replacement by compulsory labor conscriptions and draconian vagrancy laws would have ensured many like Ngeve would face Portuguese captivity in its colonies in either west-central Africa or in Brazil.[56]

54 Paul E. Lovejoy, "Civilian casualties in the context of the trans-Atlantic slave trade," in John Laband, ed., *Daily Lives of Civilians in Wartime Africa: From Slavery Days to Rwandan Genocide* (Westport, CT: Greenwood Press, 2007), 44 fn. 37; Paul E. Lovejoy, "The Provenance of Catherine Mulgrave Zimmermann: Methodological Considerations," Harriet Tubman Seminar, October 12, 2010 (http://harriet.tubman1 .yorku.ca/sites/default/files/Lovejoy_Provenance_of_Catherine_Mulgrave_ Zimmermann.pdf), p. 1; Ulrike Sill, *Encounters in Quest of Christian Womanhood: The Basel Mission in Pre- And Early Colonial Ghana* (Leiden: Brill, 2010), 111; Maureen Warner-Lewis, "Catherine Mulgrave's Unusual Transatlantic Odyssey," *Jamaica Journal* 31, nos. 1–2 (2008): 32, 42 fn. 2.

55 Zimmermann to Basel Mission Headquarters, dated 18 November 1852, Usu [Accra], in Lovejoy, "Provenance," pp. 11–12. Transcribed by Peter Haenger, this German letter appears in appendix A. The translation is by Kwasi Konadu.

56 On Portuguese abolitionism, see João Pedro Marques, *Sá da Bandeira e o fim da escravidão: Vitória da moral, desforra do interesse* (Lisbon: Instituto Ciencias Sociais, 2008). On Nbena's story, see José C. Curto, "The Story of Nbena, 1817–1820: Unlawful Enslavement and the Concept of 'Original Freedom' in Angola," in Paul E. Lovejoy and David V. Trotman, eds., *Trans-Atlantic Dimensions of Ethnicity in the African Diaspora* (London: Continuum, 2003), 44–60.

Somewhere in March or April 1833, Ngeve and presumably her older twin, among others, were captured by Portuguese slavers, who evaded detection by hiding the enslaved and showing inspectors, presumably a British antislaving squadron, their official documentation. The vessel then sailed for Cuba. Speaking to her second husband, Johannes Zimmermann, Ngeve tells about this moment of capture and crossing:

[A] mulatto schoolgirl thirteen years old, took her [Ngeve] and another cousin, also a mulatto schoolgirl, about 7 years old, for a walk near the sea, where they fished. An 8 year old boy, also related to the girls who also went to the school, was helping them. While they were thus playing, a boat arrived with several European sailors, who went ashore and called out to them. They were a distance away from the city and it was evening. The boy ran away immediately. The older girl listened to the promises of the sailors to give them delicious food, and the three girls were, despite some fear, carried into the boat in which the scoundrels rowed away; the girls had lost their appetite and they started to scream but in vain; they were brought unto *one of the many anchored ships*, where the captain received them very friendly in his cabin. The ship departed on the same night. In the cabin they found a handcuffed mulatto woman from the same city who cried bitterly, of course the girls did too. The captain tried to console them, whereby this mulatto woman acted as interpreter. The next morning the land had disappeared.[57]

This Portuguese schooner called the *Heroina* and led by captain João Sabin was shipwrecked on or just before April 20, 1833; as the schooner broke in two and sank with its captives to a "watery grave," Ngeve recalled (in Johannes's words) "the slaves screamed and moaned, the captain wept, the sailors ate and drank." The surviving girls (and a few others) found their way to Jamaica and eventually to Kingston, where they were put under the care of the Custom House Officers. At some point two of the sisters were separated from the third, but we are not told which one, since the governor Constantine Henry Phipps (the second Earl of Mulgrave in 1812) and his wife took Ngeve, a sister or cousin of hers, and a boy to their residence in Spanish Town, Jamaica. The two girls, Ngeve (renamed Catherine Mulgrave) and her sister or cousin (renamed Susan Mulgrave), were sent to the Female Refuge School ran by the Moravians when the governor and his wife left Jamaica in March 1834. Susan was also referred to as Sarah, and she became Susan Wilson by marriage, while Ngeve graduated from the

---

[57] Ibid., 12 (emphasis added).

school and became a teacher through the Mico Normal Teaching Institution in Kingston. On December 11, 1832, Ngeve married George Thompson, an African unordained missionary school teacher who hailed from Cape Mount on the Kru coast (now Liberia).[58] In 1843, 11 Basel missionaries posted at Christiansborg (Osu) on the Gold Coast died of tropical disease, and, subsequently, the Basel Mission headquarter and the Moravian Church of Jamaica headquartered in Germany agreed on a scheme to recruit "ex-slave Christians" from Jamaica for the Gold Coast. That year, 23 or 25 "ex-slave Christians," including Ngeve, left for the Gold Coast. Soon, two mission schools were founded in Christiansborg – a girls' school by Ngeve and a boys' school by George Thompson. Ngeve would suffer several miscarriages and two of her children would die in infancy, while her husband George would become riddled with drunkenness and extramarital affairs, eventually leading to a divorce and George's early departure from the Basel mission community. Ngeve would raise their two children, remain at Christiansborg, and become well versed in the Gã language and in local culture. She married Johannes Zimmerman—against the wishes of the Basel leadership in Europe—in 1851. That year, only 46 "black Christians" were counted among the Basel mission community, 25 of which were "West Indian volunteers" or "repatriates," among them Ngeve. As Jon Miller has noted, three kinds of individuals were drawn to the mission: local rulers in matrilineal societies who wanted their children to have the perceived advantage of European schooling; formerly enslaved individuals whose bonds could be broken when the mission "bought them free" and who were received in its Christian community; and widows and others (orphans, outcasts, deserted women, those with deformities).[59] A decade later, the Basel mission community on the Gold Coast consisted of 12 African employees who were Christians but slaveholders, 11 slaveholders, 33 Christian slaves with Christian holders, 209 "heathen slaves" with Christian holders, and 5 Christian slaves with "heathen" holders.[60] If this picture of a missionary community on the Gold Coast seems strange and deeply incompatible, we can imagine the communities outside of it during the

---

[58] Zimmermann to Basel Mission Headquarters, in Lovejoy, "Provenance," p. 13; Warner-Lewis, "Unusual Transatlantic Odyssey," 35–37, 43 fn. 29.

[59] Jon Miller, *Missionary Zeal and Institutional Control: Organizational Contradictions in the Basel Mission on the Gold Coast, 1828–1917* (Grand Rapids, Mich., and London: Eerdmans and RoutledgeCurzon, 2003), 23.

[60] Ibid., 149.

mid-nineteenth century when official reports to the British parliament argued that slavery had not disappeared but had taken on different forms in British African settlements in West Africa.[61]

As a member of that contrasting and even paradoxical community, Ngeve would later succumb to pneumonia and make her transition on January 14, 1891. At the time of Ngeve's passing, such communities were becoming common fixtures on the western and eastern hemispheres of Africa, and in its northern, central and southern quadrants. As individuals, especially women and children, were being uprooted and subjected to forms of servitude, older women like Ngeve became the foremost evangelists and, for central and southern people, "widows and isolated women became the preponderant element in the early Christian church."[62] Indeed, the very existence of missionary patrons with antislavery convictions and the capacity to grant refuge through Christian communities was significant, but to a thematic point. The constellation of family and community still loomed large, as it did before and during transatlantic slaving, and now "freedom" often meant family, for women in particular wanted to be reunited with kin and close friends, often in a cultural homeland. Missionaries, with their own ideas about community, were often displeased that their ideas of freedom were not acceptable to African women who lived with them as "liberated slaves" and who admitted such women still felt as "slaves" so as long they had not returned home to their relatives.[63]

As the nineteenth century came to a close, virtually all transatlantic slaving in the Atlantic region came to end and its foremost icon—the slave ship—retired from that line of labor and many of the viable ones were transformed, yet again, into commercial vessels under new ownership. On the African continent and in the African diaspora forged in the Americas, the story was quite different. In the eastern portions of Africa, international slaving and domestic seizures and captivities persisted in the lives of Yusuf and Sanqur bin Abdul Khair of Bagamoyo, Mabrook (an Ngindo), Faraj (40-year-old Makua), Suedi and Nasiboo (17- and 18-year-old Yao), Shereefah (20-year-old Nyasa), Khamsini (24-year-old Yao), Hidayah (22-year-old Nyasa), Toombo (19-year-old Yao), and Walaid bin Mulla (40-year-old of

[61] Richard Robert Maddan, *The Memoirs (chiefly autobiographical) from 1798 to 1886 of Richard Robert Madden* (London: Ward & Downey, 1891), 112–17.
[62] Marcia Wright, *Strategies of Slaves & Women: Life-Stories from East/Central Africa* (New York and London: Lilian Barber Press and James Currey, 1993), 166.
[63] Ibid., 172.

Ukambani, eastern Kenya).[64] In northern and western Africa, the same could be said, especially when explored through the experiences of Fatma Bakra of Timbuktu and Morocco and Alfred Diban of Da in present-day Burkina Faso, who served his holder in Timbuktu only to be aided by a Catholic mission in his escape. He was baptized somewhere in 1901 and became a key proselyte.[65] In northeast Africa, captives such as Djalo of Tumale (Sudan), Akafede of Ethiopia, and Josephine Bakhita of the Sudan were not uncommon, especially during the years of the Mahdist or Anglo-Sudan War (ca. 1881–1899), when Josephine was ceded from a Turkish general to the Italian Consul in Khartoum. The Consul agreed to take her to Italy, and there she decided to stay and eventually became a Catholic nun.[66] In the Americas, the story of 10-year-old Dodo, a "liberated" African in Havana unlawfully consigned to a 15-year apprenticeship only to be imprisoned in northern Morocco for protesting his unjust captivity, was not uncommon either.[67] Other "liberated" Africans consigned to the West India regiments were sentenced to penal servitude in Australia, breaking rocks and carting timber.[68] Throughout their collected stories, the fragility of freedom and of captivity was as clear as their desires for belonging and community and, for many, a cultural homeland.

---

[64] Edward A. Alpers and Matthew S. Hopper, "Parler en son nom? Comprendre les témoignages d'esclaves africains originaires de l'océan Indien (1850–1930)," *Annales: Histoire, Sciences Sociales* 63, no. 3 (2008): 808, 812, 817–26.

[65] E. Ann McDougall, "A Sense of Self: The Life of Fatma Barka," *Canadian Journal of African Studies* 32, no. 2 (1998): 285–315; Joseph Ki-Zerbo, *Alfred Diban: Premier chretien de Haute-Volta* (Paris: Editions du Cerf, 1983).

[66] Janet J. Ewald, *Soldiers, Traders, and Slaves: State Formation and Economic Transformation in the Greater Nile Valley, 1700–1885* (Madison: University of Wisconsin Press, 1990), 3, 10; P. E. H. Hair, "The Brothers Tutschek and Their Sudanese Informants," *Sudan Notes and Records* 50 (1969): 61–62; Maria Luisa Dagnino, *Bakhita Tells Her Story*, 3rd ed. (Rome: Canossiane Figlie della Carità, 1993): 37–68.

[67] Oscar Grandio Moraguez, "Dobo: A Liberated African in Nineteenth-Century Havana," http://www.slavevoyages.org/tast/assessment/essays-grandio.faces (accessed December 5, 2012).

[68] See the forthcoming work by Cassandra Pybus, "A Return to Bondage: African-American Convicts Transported to Australia," in *Global Conversations: New Scholarship on the History of Black People*, soon to be published by the University of Illinois Press, and by Reena N. Goldthree of Dartmouth College on the subject of soldiers from the Caribbean sent to the penal colony of Australia.

TOWARD CALCULATING
THE UNQUANTIFIABLE

If "man's liberty is an illusion," which a Fula sold into North African slavery named Griga argued at the end of the nineteenth century, then how do we come to terms with the global enslavement and journeys of liberation from it among a cast of African peoples?[69] For Griga and so many others, the voyage from community to captivity and through various ecologies and by sea (of water or sand) remained endless. Transatlantic slaving was set in motion by a set of human actions and coincidences that together gave birth to and fed a creature called global capitalism. This capitalism, in a myriad of ways, defines our present standing in historical time and is violently trespassing on the days after tomorrow. The pursuit of capital or prestige turned humans into commodities and properties that could be cannibalized or liquidated for labor and, for the waiting missionary, their souls. This is not to argue that these processes were novel. They existed in ancient times, but certainly not on the same global scales, using the same machines and instruments of terror, rationalized by the same kinds of cultural-religious claims, and violently marrying what became Africa, Europe, and the Americas. Perhaps these regions of the world would have engaged in a different kind of courtship, but the forced marriage occasioned by transatlantic slaving made this alternative scenario still difficult to contemplate. Rather than limit it, the transatlantic slave system and overseas slavery extended Europe's reach into Africa and the Americas, forever transforming both world regions in comparative and distinct ways. Driven by European credit on all sides of the Atlantic and into the western Indian Ocean, wealth was amassed by most, except the enslaved. The major European slaving nations and their neo-European societies in the Americas dumped their tobacco, rum, textile, iron, and weapons on African societies linked to Atlantic slaving, and some members of those societies used these goods locally to gain or maintain status and political authority of some sort. In Britain and not elsewhere in Europe, mercantilism and slavery provided this leading slaving nation with free arable land and labor overseas, allowing it to transition—sooner than others— from mercantilism to industrial capitalism and allowing for the sufficient accumulation of capital to finance technological and banking

---

[69] John Hunwick and Eve Troutt Powell, *The African diaspora in the Mediterranean lands of Islam* (Princeton, N.J.: Markus Wiener, 2002), 218.

innovations and the production of raw material worldwide. For large tracts of African land and its inhabitants, their transition, if we can call it that, was more of the same: widening commerce in nonhuman resources procured by captives put to local production, deepened mistrust and vulnerabilities, and the quest for kin- or community-based refuge from it all, including Christian communities originating from the leading European slaving nations that created or facilitated those insecurities. Rather than a coming to terms with the human costs of transatlantic slaving, abolitionism and "legitimate trade" simply reorganized the unequal power and labor relations charted by international and overseas slavery.

In recent history, coming to terms with the impacts of transatlantic, much less western Indian Ocean, slaving has often meant some kind of redress, reconciliation, or repair on account of the human costs involved during and the collateral damages after the transatlantic era. In Marcus Rediker's *The Slave Ship*, in the closing section entitled "Dead Reckoning," he raises the question of reparations—"a different accounting"—by arguing that "justice demands that it be posed—and answered, if the legacy of slavery is ever to be overcome. There can be no reconciliation without justice."[70] But he qualifies this question, steering the onus away from the historian, himself and others, and toward "a social movement for justice, led by the descendants of those who have suffered most from the legacy of the slave trade, slavery, and the racism they spawned, joined by allies in a broader struggle to end continuity operation of capitalism."[71] However, a "social movement" against *what* and against *whom*? If the target is capitalism, this ghost of "violence and terror" operates through human action, which then points to a group of people called capitalists. But which capitalists? Are they the "descendants of [James] D'Wolf, [Humphry] Morice, and [Henry] Laurens—their families, their class, their government, and the societies they helped to construct," as Rediker seem to suggest? Rediker equivocates and, for one reason or another, is less than clear about the very tough questions he raises.[72] In *Imperial Reckoning*, historian Caroline Elkins focuses on the terrorism of British colonial rule in Kenya, and, on estimating the Gĩkũyũ or Kikuyu casualties, she argues, "of course,

---

[70] Marcus Rediker, *The Slave Ship: A Human History* (New York: Penguin, 2007), 353.

[71] Ibid., 354–55.

[72] Ibid., 353.

we will never know exactly how many Kikuyu died during the last years of British colonial rule in Kenya. But does this matter? The impact of the detention camps and villages goes well beyond statistics."[73] Certainly, a similar case could be made for the African and diasporic causalities of transatlantic slavery, but what about the matter of "reckoning" so central to Elkins's project and apparently to Rediker's? Though calls for "compensation" were made in the wake of Kenya's political independence, there have yet to be an "official reconciliation" process, and only recently has a landmark court case been initiated by survivors of those detention camps in the British judiciary system—and where Elkins is an expert witness.[74] Though historians cannot adjudicate the "past," they, as Elkins demonstrates, can and should play an integral role in national and international processes of reconciliation, redress, and repair by marshaling the best of what they currently know, especially anchored in the experiences and perspectives of the enslaved and their progenies and at the scale of households and villages.

But how do we come to terms with historic enslavement of African and diasporic peoples using documentary and oral records, often atomized into statistics or painful memories, that lie and tell the truth simultaneously? In other words, the popularity of quantification and statistic studies that focus on slave prices, volume, supply, cargo, tonnage, losses, and profit tells us quite a bit about the structural workings of transatlantic slaving but much less about the identities, interior lives, and social realities of the individuals and families concerned. Further, quantification, which is central to any argument for monetary redress, has its numerous and overlapping virtues and vices. In a fascinating study by Nathan Nunn and Leonard Wantchekon, the two economists argue that contemporary individuals whose ancestors were brought into Atlantic and Indian Ocean slaving show low levels of trust in their neighbors, relatives, other cultural groups, and their local governments on account of the "slave trade," suggesting the latter's impact reached not only households but also cultural norms, core beliefs, and values. This "culture of mistrust" and "400 years of insecurity," however insightful, cannot be reduced to a number or set of numbers, which causes accounting problems for those seeking fiscal redress. The same is true for cultural norms or core values: How does one

[73] Caroline Elkins, *Imperial Reckoning: The Untold Story of Britain's Gulag in Kenya* (New York: Henry Holt, 2005), 366.
[74] Ibid., 367.

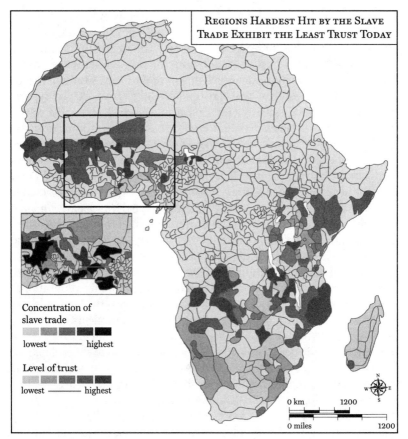

REGIONS HARDEST HIT BY THE SLAVE
TRADE EXHIBIT THE LEAST TRUST TODAY

Concentration of
slave trade

lowest ——— highest

Level of trust

lowest ——— highest

0 km   1200

0 miles   1200

MAP 3 African Distrust and the Slave Trade

measure these qualitative factors and assign to one or all a monetary
value?[75]

Some readers will no doubt point out the case of the African
woman whom we know only as Belinda in late eighteenth-century
Massachusetts who filed more than one court petition for redress and
was compensated, at least in one instance, for her years of enslavement. But cases like hers were unexceptional at that time, and her
petition was for personal rather than collective "reparations." More

---

[75] Nathan Nunn and Leonard Wantchekon, "The Slave Trade and the Origins of
Mistrust in Africa," *American Economic Review* 101, no. 7 (2011): 3249–52.

recent court cases for African American reparations rest on moral and legal arguments for "unjust enrichment," but these cases and their proponents have yet to make clear their ultimate goals.[76] Is an apology, a payoff (lump sum or installation), or race relations the only or most effective way to frame reparations? What forms would or should reparations take? What would recipients do if they received reparations? Who would be eligible for reparations? Which slavery or slaveries and which African diaspora could qualify? What kind or set of evidences would be drawn together to buttress the case for whatever kind of reparation is sought? And is it sensible to pursue and expect redress in the highest courts of the nations that would be on trial? These are neither idle nor academic questions, and they are not restricted to North America. In some parts of Africa, the call for reparations has gained some traction, and in the Caribbean, the president of Antigua has called for reparations from the United States, while Jamaica has recently revived its reparations commission to seek compensation or a formal apology from Britain "to heal old wounds." This same commission is charged with developing a "financial estimate for reparations," which is viewed as "critical to coming to terms with the lasting legacy of slavery."[77] In a very ironic way, the kind of arithmetic used to transform captive Africans into kinless commodities a few centuries ago is being evoked to once more reassign monetary value to those departed souls so that some undefined group(s) can get their just enrichment in the present. It remains unclear if this is the "different accounting" Rediker had in mind or if Elkins's book and testimony will pay off for those in Kenya seeking redress, but it is difficult to fathom how any apology "heal[s] old wounds" or how the presence or absence of "financial" reparations could bring one "to terms with the legacy of slavery" without engaging the underpinning issues and questions at stake for those concerned.

---

[76] Charles J. Ogletree, "Repairing the Past: New Efforts in the Reparations Debate in America," *Harvard Civil Rights-Civil Liberties Law Review* 38 (2003): 279–320; Eric J. Miller, "Reconceiving Reparations: Multiple Strategies in the Reparations Debate," *Boston College Third World Law Journal* 24 (2004): 45–79.

[77] Jon Miller and Rahul Kumar, eds., *Reparations: Interdisciplinary Inquiries* (New York: Oxford University Press, 2007); Rhoda E. Howard-Hassmann and Anthony P. Lombardo, *Reparations to Africa* (Philadelphia: University of Pennsylvania Press, 2008); David McFadden, "Jamaica Revives Slavery Reparations Commission," *Associated Press*, November 1, 2012, http://bigstory.ap.org/article/jamaica-revives-slavery-reparations-commission.

FURTHER READINGS

Harms, Robert, David W. Blight, and Bernard K. Freamon, eds. *Indian Ocean Slavery in the Age of Abolition.* New Haven, Conn.: Yale University Press, 2013.

Inikori, Joseph E., and Stanley L. Engerman, eds. *The Atlantic Slave Trade: Effects on Economies, Societies and Peoples in Africa, the Americas, and Europe.* Durham, N.C.: Duke University Press, 1992.

Nunn, Nathan, and Leonard Wantchekon. "The Slave Trade and the Origins of Mistrust in Africa." *American Economic Review* 101, no. 7 (2011): 3221–52.

Nunn, Nathan. "The Long-Term Effects of Africa's Slave Trades." *Quarterly Journal of Economics* 123, no. 1 (2008): 139–76.

Pierce, Lamar, and Jason Snyder. *The Historical Roots of Firm Access to Finance: Evidence from the African Slave Trade* (January 1, 2013). Available at SSRN: http://ssrn.com/abstract=2185146.

Epilogue

Almost Home: Forgetful Memories and Getting the Stories Right

There is a scene at the end of the movie *Amistad* in which a British admiral assaults the fort from which Sengbeh Pieh and his fellow Africans had been sold into slavery years before. The message is unequivocal—slavery is something of the past. It occupies a discrete section in American history textbooks, ending neatly in 1865. Elsewhere, huge events are planned to memorialize the bicentennials of the 1807 British abolition of the slave trade, the annual recognition of "Juneteenth"—the day the British Empire outlawed slavery—and the sesquicentennial of the 1848 French abolition of slavery in its colonies. These "ends" are necessary for the story of the Atlantic slave trade to fit into the narrative of progress and the upward path from barbarism to modernity that comprises the dominant historical narrative given for much of the Atlantic world. As societies that worship "freedom" and "civil rights," we must acknowledge our dark past but then shut it away safely.

Yet slavery did not end with the imposition of laws and through the actions of naval squadrons. Abolition did not put an end to servitude. Manumission did not miraculously cure the damage done by enslavement. Emancipation was not a panacea for the ills caused by the slaving system. Nor can the slavery of the past be neatly packaged into an official or academic "history" and then placed to the side as if it doesn't have any legacy in the minds of individuals, the collective memories of societies, and the organization of communities and states today.

For that reason, we chose not to close this book with a conclusion that "ends" the story, but rather with an exploration of the ways in which the Atlantic slaving system continues to resonate and affect us today. This is not an exploration of where slavery still exists today, although it's clear that the experiences of enslavement are still to be found on some rural plantations and in some urban households. Rather, we want to continue to focus on the massive forced migration of the Atlantic slaving system by looking at the ways in which it is still known, understood, and dealt with in popular culture on both sides of the Atlantic. We will ask three important questions: How do Atlantic societies and especially diasporic and continental African societies choose to remember the Atlantic slaving system today? What are the contests and debates about how that past should be remembered, or alternately forgotten, and what do they tell us about our own society? Finally, what should the relationship be between works of history like this book and popular memories of the Atlantic slaving system?

HISTORY AND ITS ALTERNATIVES

The Atlantic slave system has been a subject of study for historians for well over a century. In textbooks, articles, and popular histories meant for wide audiences, professional historians made use of the journals of slave traders, the writing of abolitionists, the narratives of former slaves, and later quantitative records from ship's captains and companies involved in the trade to ask how the system started, how it functioned, and why it ended. However, for much of the nineteenth and twentieth centuries, the parts of the Atlantic world rich enough to fund professional historians—Europe and North America especially— paid little attention to the history of Africans generally and the Atlantic slaving system specifically. In the 1960s this began to change through the pressure of both newly independent west and west-central

African states and diasporic African communities. By the late 1970s, the study of the Atlantic slaving system was burgeoning through the efforts of scholars like Joseph Inikori and Philip Curtin. Over time, the field grew large enough that it could encompass many subfields. Today, these include social and cultural history, which emphasized the experiences and perspectives of the enslaved and the communities from which they came and which they built in the Americas. Historians are also producing a large body of scholarship that carefully interprets the great amount of quantitative data amassed under the leadership of historians David Eltis, Stephen Behrendt, Manolo Florentino, David Richardson, and others. It is through their work and the textbooks based on their analyses that most North and South Americans, Europeans, and even many Africans formally learn about the slave trade in school.

In general, at least until the last few years, the historical analysis of the Atlantic slaving system has been conducted largely through the rules, methods, and theories of the discipline of history. Most of these studies are designed to appear objective and scholarly rather than passionate and involved. Historians are supposed to keep their own views out of their research and never use the pronoun "I." They base their findings on evidence, but not all evidence is given equal weight. Generally, written documents from archives have more weight than archaeological finds, which carry more weight than folktales, proverbs, and knowledge passed down by word of mouth. The avowed intent of history is not to carry a particular message or moral, but rather to tell the past "as it actually happened."

Guided by these rules, historians have tended to ask specific questions about the Atlantic slaving system. They strive to understand how and why it started, who was involved, and how it functioned. They look at it as part of long trends in African, Atlantic, and American history. They try to understand the immediate impact of the system on societies in different parts of the world. Finally, some historians focus on what it felt like to be captured, to cross the Atlantic, or to live as an enslaved African in a new society.

This is important information, but it does not necessarily give us a complete picture of the place that the Atlantic slaving system holds in both human history and contemporary society. Very few histories produced by professional historians really address the ongoing reverberations of the slave system in contemporary society and daily life. Few focus on the messages that the enslaved and societies involved in the trade might have tried to pass on to later generations. Nor do they generally reflect the ways in which those descendants keep alive knowledge about that past or repress it.

This does not mean that doing academic history is a bad or useless act. Rather, it means that in order to understand the Atlantic slaving system and the ways in which people of later generations relate to it, we need to go beyond history. This is entirely possible, because history isn't the only way of knowing the past. In fact, people who aren't historians and even those who don't read history texts generally know of the past in a variety of ways. We can create a typology of these alternatives to history, although they overlap somewhat. The first and most inclusive is *memory*. Memory refers primarily to psychically retained and interpreted accounts of first-person experiences in the past, often collected and expressed as "oral histories." These memories are "archived" in individuals, although, as Steve Stern has argued, they have the potential to coalesce in "knots" and "albums" that allow them to be shared and used. *Nostalgia* is a particular type of memory, referring to sentimental understandings of the past that emerge in times of crisis and that frequently find political and social expression in conservative movements (i.e., movements against change). *Tradition* is somewhat different from memory in that it is more commonly collective and also practiced. Tradition is usually a means by which groups construct their identity by reference to a shared past. Traditions generally center around practice—"doing something"—and can therefore be found in certain rituals and sites that reflect a shared past and identity. Nostalgia, memory, and tradition all find expression in the practices of *heritage*: an organized paradigm and set of rituals, sites, and understandings of the past through which collective identity is shaped. Heritage can be "global," for example, through the United Nations Educational, Scientific, and Cultural Organization's (UNESCO) identification of certain places as "World Heritage Sites." However, it is more often localized and exclusive. People embrace heritage as something innate to their group. In the contemporary world, heritage is often embodied in formal institutions that are formed to "preserve" and "celebrate" a national or communal past.

All of these ways of looking at the past have relevance for the way that people understand the Atlantic slaving system and its repercussions. Memories of the slave trade are retained through rumors, proverbs, and family narratives that usually convey some message about how it was experienced. Traditions like rituals, songs, and dances are often also used to carry on messages about the system and its impact. Heritage sites like slave forts and plantations are preserved by UNESCO,

FIGURE 6   Slave route monument in Benin. The monument commemorates the Africans exported from their homelands during the transatlantic slaving era. The monument is situated along the "Road of the Slaves" in the West African country of Benin. (Photo by Kwasi Konadu.)

national government, or local groups. On the other hand, there is little nostalgia for the period of the Atlantic slaving system, as it is not remembered as a positive thing. Rather, there are many silences about the period.

Many historians recognize that if we want to understand the Atlantic slaving system and its impact, we must look at heritage, tradition, and memory. However, these ways of knowing the past are not entirely compatible with the discipline of history. Unlike formal history, these ways of knowing the past are meant to be subjective, personal, and passionate. They are meant to embrace messages that are "authentic" rather than to necessarily prove their accuracy using evidence. Thus history and its alternatives sometimes clash in the pursuit of understandings of the Atlantic slaving system. At the heart of this debate is the question of the purpose of studying the system and the "truth" we should take away from it. This issue came to a head in the 1990s on Gorée Island. Gorée was a Portuguese and French settlement partly because of the Atlantic system, and the island has several sites of commemoration, including a major museum in the Fort d'Estrees. Historians have also written extensively about slavery in Gorée. The evidence they have compiled shows that the island had a large enslaved population at times—a 1785 census lists 1250 slaves alongside about 800 free inhabitants, of whom 10 percent were European. Yet for the most part these captives were permanent workers on the island rather than meant for export across the Atlantic. In fact, the records recovered and used by historians suggest that very few enslaved Africans left the continent through Gorée—no more than 500 per year at the height of the trade. This was partly because it didn't make sense to transship captives from the Senegambian mainland to an island before sending them on again to the Americas, but also because the export trade from northern Senegal decreased earlier than in other regions due to local choice.

Nevertheless, Gorée was designated a UNESCO World Heritage Site in 1980 partly as a place of remembrance of the Atlantic slave trade and soon after began to experience a rise in visitors, especially Africans of the diaspora, seeking to reconnect with their past and understand the system that had brought their ancestors to the Americas. The central site of their visits was the Maison des Esclaves, a Gorée house with a dark basement and a door "of no return" leading out to the sea. The curator of the house, Joseph N'Diaye, began to give tours of the house in which he stated that tens of millions of enslaved Africans had passed through Gorée and that the basement had been a dungeon for storing many of these captives. In a 1995 contribution to an online discussion, historian Philip Curtin responded that not only were these numbers outrageous but that the basement of the house had been for storing goods only. A number of African scholars, mostly nonhistorians, responded that the exact numbers and history of the house were unimportant. Achille Mbembe wrote that the actual number of humans who passed through the island as captives were "mere decoration," and added that scholarship on the slave trade had been misleading "precisely because of this obsession with numbers." Gloria Emeagwali wrote to compare Gorée with "the Vietnam War Memorial or other monuments of the dead."[1] At a conference that followed, Senegalese scholar Djibril Samb lauded Joseph N'Diaye for "leading a fine battle of memory," even while most participants recognized that the numbers he quoted were not strictly accurate.[2] History and heritage were

---

[1] http://www.h-net.org/~africa/threads/goree.html.

[2] Ralph A. Austen, "The Slave Trade as History and Memory: Confrontations of Slaving Voyage Documents and Communal Traditions," *The William and Mary Quarterly*, 58 (2001): 229–244.

thus in conflict on this island. One emphasized the "truth" of evidence and facts, while another put forward metaphors and messages about the horror of the experiences of the enslaved meant to instruct popes and presidents as well as pilgrims from across the Atlantic. Both had something of value, and both had limitations in what they could express and the role they could play. Also, the two ways of understanding the past acted as a sort of a check on each other, pointing out the moral limits of looking at numbers and the real issues in being inaccurate. In this way, history and its alternatives function together to help us to understand the past and its repercussions in our own society.

MEMORY AND SILENCE

For individuals and societies who experienced the Atlantic slaving system, of course, no history textbook or official heritage was needed. Rather, their own memories functioned to remind them of their experiences. These memories not only affected their actions but also were in many cases passed down to future generations. Unfortunately, it is difficult for scholars to find out about these memories. In many cases, they were not recorded and were lost, sometimes through neglect or error and sometimes on purpose. In other cases, scholars just don't have easy access to communal and individual memories that are intensely personal or emotionally and politically charged.

Among the few firsthand individual memories of the Atlantic slaving system that were recorded were narratives written by former slaves who had emancipated themselves or had been liberated. These include Africans of the diaspora like Venture Smith and Gustavus who were literate, often hooked up with abolitionist groups, and frequently published their stories in order to attack the slave trade.[3] They also include Africans like Lydia Yawo and Aaron Kuku who escaped slavery and joined religious communities in the Gold Coast. In both cases, their memories were frequently recorded as narratives of their conversion to Christianity. Thus they often take on religious overtones, such as remembering slavery as "Egyptian bondage" or "Babylonian exile," and comparing emancipation with religious conversion as a

[3] Venture Smith, *A Narrative of the Life and Adventures of Venture, a Native of Africa But resident above sixty years in the United States of America. Related by Himself* (New London, Conn.: Charles Holt, 1798). Olaudah Equiano, *The Interesting Narrative of the Life of Olaudah Equiano, or Gustavus Vassa, the African. Written by Himself* (London, 1789).

form of redemption. Those that were specifically written or published to combat slavery also often stressed evidence of individual suffering.[4] Other evidence of firsthand memories of the Atlantic slaving sytem are hard to find and decode, although as we have seen in earlier chapters, the system was sometimes remembered through the idioms of witchcraft and cannibalism.

Over time, of course, firsthand individual memories were silenced, often unrecorded, as individuals died. What remained were communal memories that were passed down through traditions such as stories, songs such as funeral dirges, performances, and other rituals. Usually, the traditions that survived involved some performance and poetry, and often props, meant to help with memorization. Sometimes there are professional "rememberers" involved. In Sierra Leone, the bloody and dangerous period of the slave trade gave rise to a class of diviners whose job it was to protect people through religious intervention. The diviners developed rituals that encapsulated the dangers of a period meant to keep people safe in an increasingly unsafe world. Those rituals remain in use today to protect people from other challenges. The diviners now serve politicians and merchants, giving them spiritual support in their jobs and helping them avoid the jealousy of competitors through these rituals. Although the Atlantic slaving system is seldom specifically invoked in the rituals, they are themselves in many ways memories of the violence done by the trade.

In other cases, memories are passed down privately but are commonly known. For example, Sandra Greene and Anne Bailey have looked at narratives from the Anlo-Ewe town of Atorkor, which was a trading point where captives from the interior were sold to slave traders. Stories are still passed down firsthand of an event that began when relatives and officers of the local paramount chief were invited on board a slave-trading ship, offered drinks, and then seized as slaves themselves. The basic message of this story was that "nobody was safe" during that period. Many people know of this story, but they usually learn of it privately through stories told by elders. In Nigeria, as in many other places, memories of slavery are usually something passed down within families rather than talked about publicly. Many people know about family members who were enslaved, about the ways in

[4] See especially Sandra Greene, *West African Narratives of Slavery: Texts from Late Nineteenth- and Early Twentieth-Century Ghana* (Bloomington: Indiana University Press, 2011). Also Audrey Fisch, ed., *The Cambridge Companion to The African American Slave Narrative* (Cambridge, U.K.: Cambridge University Press, 2007).

which enslavement operated and the routes of slavery, and about its impact on their ancestors' lives. An increasing number of African scholars studying these issues, sometimes from within their own communities—like G. Ugo Nwokeji—have been able to bring to light oral accounts demonstrating that knowledge about the slaving system, while not talked about publicly, is deeply ingrained in the sorts of stories people tell in a familial setting.[5] Ethnographers Paolo Gaibazzi and Benedetta Rossi are also partnering with elders in Gambia and Niger to explore the ways that dependency and inequality survived the official abolition of slavery, even to affecting social relationships and lived experiences today.[6]

Across the Atlantic, memories of the Atlantic slave system are often more public. In the Caribbean, those who fought against slavery are often reflected in popular memory. In Guadeloupe, the rebel captives Ignace and Louis Delgrès appear as murals on many walls and in popular songs and poems. In Brazil, memory made its way onto television in the wildly popular 1990s miniseries *Escrava Anastácia* (which remains a very popular YouTube offering). This story followed the life of a young noblewoman born in Nigeria who experienced the Middle Passage and the horrors of enslavement yet also embodies the continuing African religious and cultural heritage of Brazilians today.

At the same time, however, memories and traditions dealing with the Atlantic slaving system have in many places been officially suppressed, purposefully forgotten, or silenced through the decisions of individuals and families not to talk about this part of their past. These silences probably exist for several reasons. Perhaps most importantly, silences evolve to allow situations to take place that technically contravene supposed social rules. In many places in Africa today, the children of former slaves hold power despite the stigma of slavery. Also, in some places the descendants of slaves and slave owners or slavers have to live together despite their histories. This can only happen because of silences. By contrast, talking about slavery is socially disruptive. It can also be politically disruptive. In Ghana, silences to some degree protect national integrity since there are radically different understandings

---

[5] G. Ugo Nwokeji, *The Slave Trade and Culture in the Bight of Biafra: An African Society in the Atlantic World* (New York: Cambridge University Press, 2010).

[6] Paolo Gaibazzi, "Two Soninke 'Slave' Descendants and Their Family Biographies" and Benedetta Rossi, "Without History? Interrogating 'Slave' Memories in Ader (Niger)," in Alice Bellagamba, Sandra E. Greene, and Martin A. Klein, eds., *African Voices on Slavery and the Salve Trade* (New York: Cambridge University Press, 2013), 522–535, 536–554.

of the slave trade in different regions and slavery is also a factor in struggles for power and chieftaincy disputes.

Sometimes communities suppress memories of the Atlantic slaving system because they want to assimilate. This is especially true in diasporic African minorities, who feel the need to be seen as "modern" and equal and therefore silence parts of their history. Similarly, in parts of Africa, those descended from former slaves desire to not be seen as having a "slave background" because it still connotes low status. In some cases accusations that political leaders are descended from slaves are still used in political campaigns to suggest that they are "illegitimate" leaders.

In some parts of Europe and the Americas, it is the government or powerful elites who suppress discussion of the Atlantic slaving system as part of the history of a region. For example, former slave-worked plantations like the Musée du Rhum and Oak Alley in Louisiana as well as fine houses in Charleston, South Carolina, give guided tours that say little about the history of slavery. Their owners and guides seem to feel that this history disrupts the nostalgia of a "finer past" of masked balls and gentry living. Similarly, slavery generally has no place in tours of the houses of the celebrated national forefathers. Speaking too extensively about Thomas Jefferson's ownership of slaves, for example, seems to contradict the narrative that he was a leader of liberty.

Not all are satisfied with this silencing of the past that deals with the Atlantic slaving system and its impact. Writer Toni Morrison, for example, has called for "rememory"—the active recovery of the memory of the past that has been suppressed. Morrison has argued that the past reverberates even when we try to silence it, and thus communities should instead actively engage it. There are real legacies of slavery that are whispered or go unacknowledged, and they should instead be dealt with. Rememory includes official acts such as reparations, official apologies, and the building of national museums and archives but could also involve grass-roots efforts to revive traditions and stories about the past that give meaning to the present.

One recent example of rememory goes back to the story of the *Amistad* and again involves Sierra Leone. As we have seen, this country is a logical place for a sense of nation to be built at least partly around the history of the Atlantic slaving system as well as the struggle against slavery. Yet in general the place of both slavery and abolitionism in Sierra Leone was suppressed in the national memory throughout the twentieth century. Even the story of the *Amistad* and its captives, who both took over the slave ship and fought for their freedom in a Connecticut court, successfully returning to Sierra Leone, was suppressed. It especially had no place in the undemocratic rule of the brutal All People's Congress (APC) in the 1980s and therefore was entirely suppressed. The *Amistad* story was resurrected, however, by the Sierra Leonian playright Charlie Haffner. Haffner sought to create in Freetown a theater of relevance that would help raise consciousness. Among his first plays was *Amistad Kata Kata*, which emphasized the need to recognize the past and raised the *Amistad* rebels under Sengbeh Pieh as heroes of struggle against oppression. When, in 1992, the APC government was overthrown, crowds in Freetown, led by youths who had seen *Amistad Kata Kata*, seized upon Sengbe as a national hero and made him the symbol of the revolution. A nineteenth-century revolt against slavery was, now, connected in their minds with their own struggle for democratic rights and prosperity.[7]

OFFICIAL COMMEMORATION, TOURISM, AND HERITAGE

In some cases, of course, governments and powerful international organizations promote certain memories of the Atlantic slaving system rather than repressing them. However, just as there is a tension between silence and memory in the minds of individuals on both sides of the Atlantic, so too there exists a tension between organically developed individual and group memories of communities and official commemorations of slavery.

Many official commemorations of the Atlantic slaving system are in fact celebrations of emancipation through which governments claim to have been virtuous opponents of slavery. In the British Commonwealth, these focus on the 1834 emancipation; in France and its Caribbean dependencies, the 1848 abolition of slavery. In the British Commonwealth, for example, the August 1, 1834, emancipation is frequently commemorated. Some of these celebrations began spontaneously in the 1830s, but many were organized by governments. In France, commemorations surround the 1848 abolition of slavery by the French Republic. An especially large commemoration was held

---

[7] Iyunolu Folayan Osagie, *The Amistad Revolt: Memory, Slavery, and the Politics of Identity in the United States and Sierra Leone* (Athens: University of George Press, 2003), 105–113.

in 1998 (150 years) in France and its Caribbean departments. However, it was highly contested. French government figures like Prime Minister Lionel Jospin centered the celebration around French liberal ideas of liberty and the Enlightenment. President Jacques Chirac stated that the French abolitionists acted "in the name of humanity. They reinforced the foundations of democracy and the Republic."[8] Yet many descendants of enslaved Africans on the islands of Haiti, Guadeloupe, and Martinique rejected this emphasis on French abolitionism and avoidance of the discussion of French participation in the slave trade. They argued that the emancipation was seized by diasporic Africans, rather than given to them by liberal Frenchmen.

The Atlantic slaving system has also become commoditized in some regions as a source of tourism revenue, usually involving diasporic Africans seeking to reconnect with their continental African pasts. This type of "roots" tourism started as a grass-roots movement and in many cases remains intensely personal. The moment that launched it seems to have been the 1976 publication of Alex Haley's book *Roots* and the subsequent television miniseries watched by about 130 million Americans. Around the same time, there was a broad movement in the United States to embrace heritage visits to ancestral homelands—for example, Irish-Americans in Ireland and American Jews in Eastern Europe. These voyages, and those of African Americans to West Africa, were therefore a type of pilgrimage—a retracing of history as a way of reclaiming identity. However, they coincided with the rise of an African American middle class that had buying power, which was of course recognized by major corporations, entrepreneurs, and of course governments in Africa. All of these then became involved in roots tourism.

By the early 1990s, roots tourism was mostly organized by tour groups that heavily controlled the itinerary and limited exposure and also the breadth of development opportunities. In the United States, corporations like McDonald's that sought to raise their profile in the African American community became involved in the process. In 1994, for example, McDonald's sponsored 96 Americans to visit Senegal and the Gambia on a roots tour. Yet such tourism is not without controversy. For example, the McDonald's-sponsored tour was full of issues of negotiated identity and memory. At Gorée Island, the visitors wanted sanctity and a chance to reflect, but locals hoped to sell them memorabilia and other goods. At a ceremony in Gambia, the visitors

---

[8] Jacques Chirac, "L'humanisme est aussi une politicque," *Le Figaro*, 24 April 1998.

were given African names and welcomed back as lost children, but many had already taken African names and didn't want to be treated as children. They also rebelled against the controls of the tour guides, arguing that they wanted a more "authentic" experience.

Around the same time, roots tourism had become large scale enough that there was increasing competition within Africa for a piece of the potential profits. For example, many pilgrim-tourists visited the forts of the Ghanaian coast. Communities in northern Ghana, seeing this, sought to draw them into recreating the long overland trip from the interior to the slave forts. In the process, they worked with the Ghanaian tourism board. The results were an alteration of authentic memory. For example, the board advised locals in the northern town of Salaga to emphasize some topics rather than others. They were instructed to downplay local violence and conflicts that fed into the slave trade, some of which routed captives into local markets like Samori's state, and instead to emphasize their connections to the Atlantic coast. While this may have been good business, it had problematic repercussions for legitimate local memory.

Like the Ghanaian tourism board, UNESCO has become deeply involved in the Atlantic slaving system in the last four decades. They, too, have put their own particular spin on the way it should be remembered. As a global organization, UNESCO seeks to define the Atlantic slaving system as part of a "world heritage" whose memory belongs to the international community as a whole. In 1979, UNESCO designated a number of the slaving forts of coastal West Africa as World Heritage Sites. Then, in 1994, they launched the Slave Routes Project, meant to reverse "silences." The project includes scientific research and education. This involves conferences of scholars and museum workers, museum restoration projects, and preservation of documents as well as publication of books. It also includes the promotion of cultural tourism as a means to promote development. In the process of establishing the system as something of global importance, however, UNESCO has sometimes disenfranchised local communities. Similarly, by writing "official" histories of the slave trade through monuments and such, they have sometimes overriden local memories.

UNESCO, the needs of roots visitors, and the memories and priorities of Africans have in some cases created contests of meaning in terms of how to remember the Atlantic slaving system. One such place of contest is Elmina Castle, built by the Portuguese in the fifteenth century, an important site of the slaving system in the seventeenth and eighteenth centuries especially, and designated a World Heritage

Monument by UNESCO in 1979. The UNESCO decision funneled money toward its restoration and promoting tourism. However, the restoration effort and the rise of tourism have led to a number of debates between visitors, the local community, and UNESCO over questions that sometimes seem to be banal but actually reveal deep-seated issues of memory. UNESCO, for example, pushed to restore parts of the castle to their condition in earlier periods, but many roots visitors prefer that it be left undisturbed and undesecrated as a place of pilgrimage. Many visitors also wanted to see displays and tours of the castle that focused on the Atlantic slaving system, but local groups also wanted them to talk about the role of the castle in colonialism, as a place of the imprisonment of leaders like Asantehene Prempeh, and in issues of local development. In addition, when the castle became a UNESCO World Heritage Site, it became necessary to pay a fee to enter. This money was meant to support maintenance and development of the site. Both Ghanaians and Africans of the diaspora, however, have expressed a belief that they shouldn't have to pay to visit their own heritage. Debates like this reveal that the Atlantic slaving system still resonates in the lives of people around the world. It is because it still has meaning and because people are still grappling with its legacies that they care about such issues.

CONCLUSION

The Atlantic slaving system was an episode in human, African, and Atlantic history that opened in the 1440s and closed in the late nineteenth century. Yet it is also still alive today in society and in people's minds. This idea is perhaps best expressed by the great African American writer and social critic James Baldwin. Writing specifically on race and the legacy of slaving in the United States, Baldwin stated that "history does not refer merely, or even principally, to the past. On the contrary, the great force of history comes from the fact that we carry it within us, are unconsciously controlled by it in many ways, and history is literally present in all that we do. It could scarcely be otherwise, since it is to history that we owe our frames of reference, our identities, and our aspirations."[9]

Baldwin, of course, was using the term "history" to encompass not only academic scholarship but also memory, tradition, heritage, and

[9] James Baldwin, "The White Man's Guilt," *Ebony* 20 (1964), 47.

the resonances of the past in our daily lives. He reminds us that humans struggle with the past: we try to forget, we strive to remember, and we interpret that past consciously and unconsciously, internally and communally. This is especially true in dealing with episodes of terror and tragedy like the Atlantic slaving system, whose impact on both psyche and society in Africa and elsewhere was deeply scarring and has had long-lasting implications. Although at times individuals and communities must suppress it in order to survive, it cannot be ignored because its legacy cannot be erased. How and why it is remembered is a question of enormous significance for our contemporary world and also for the generations since the system began. For this reason, memory is essential in understanding the importance of a subject's past and that past in our present. For the historian, therefore, the study of memory is thus an essential part of our ever-present labors to get the stories right, especially for those historically silenced, and to fight against the common bacteria of forgetting those who should be remembered.

FURTHER READINGS

Akyeampong, Emmanuel. "History, Memory, Slave-Trade and Slavery in Anlo (Ghana)." *Slavery and Abolition* 22, no. 3 (2001): 1–24.

Audra Diptee, Audra, and David Trotman, eds. *Memory, Public History & Representations of the Past: Africa & Its Diasporas.* New York: Continuum Books, 2012.

Austen, Ralph A. "The Slave Trade as History and Memory: Confrontations of Slaving Voyage Documents and Communal Traditions." *The William and Mary Quarterly* 58 (2001): 229–44.

Bailey, Anne C. *African Voices of the Atlantic Slave Trade: Beyond the Silence and the Shame.* Boston: Beacon Books, 2005.

Bruner, Edward M. "Tourism in Ghana: The Representation of Slavery and the Return of the Black Diaspora." *American Anthropologist* 98 (1996): 290–304.

Greene, Sandra E. *West African Narratives of Slavery: Texts from Late Nineteenth- and Early Twentieth-Century Ghana.* Bloomington: Indiana University Press, 2011.

Klein, Martin A. "Studying the History of Those Who Would Rather Forget: Oral History and the Experience of Slavery." *History in Africa* 16 (1989): 209–17.

Osagie, Iyunolu Folayan. *The Amistad Revolt: Memory, Slavery, and the Politics of Identity in the United States and Sierra Leone.* Athens: University of Georgia Press, 2000.

INDEX

Note: Captives alphabetized by first name follow the style of the text